# Family Circle

# BASIC COOKING

**Albany Books**

Designed and produced by
Albany Books
36 Park Street London W1Y 4DE

First published 1979

Published by Albany Books

Copyright © Albany Books 1979

Printed in Hong Kong

ISBN 0-86136-095-8

*This text has previously been published in issues of* Family Circle. *The publishers wish to thank the Editor and staff of the magazine for their help in preparing it for this edition. They also gratefully acknowledge the loan of transparencies from* Family Circle.

*Design : Walker Pinfold Associates*
*Picture Research : Raj Sacranie*

All the recipes give both metric and imperial measurements: these conversions are not exact equivalents, so for perfect results make sure that you use either metric or imperial quantities throughout—don't mix them up.

# Contents

# Lamb

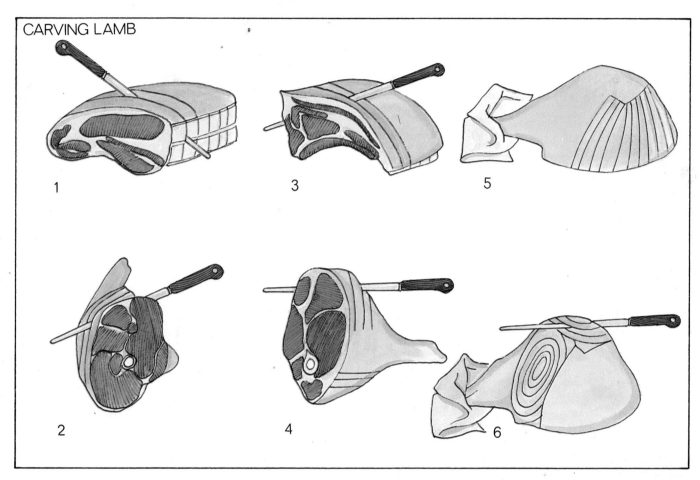

1     3     5

2     4     6

Cuts of lamb: *1. Shoulder 2. Best end of neck 3. Scrag end of neck 4. & 5. Middle neck 6. Breast 7. & 8. Loin 9. Fillet of leg 10. Shank of leg*

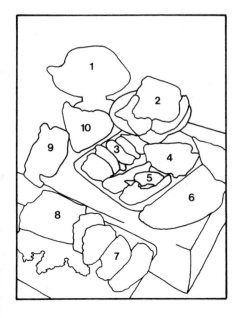

**Look for these points when buying lamb:** Lamb should always have a fine-grained appearance and be moist and pinkish. The fat should be white and firm. The choicest cuts should have some fat, with a paper-thin covering of pliable skin. Legs and shoulders should be plump with a blue tinge on knuckles and bone. Stale lamb has dark red flesh and yellow fat.

**Freezing:** Frozen lamb should not be stored in the freezer for more than twelve months.

**Cooking lamb:** Lamb joints should be roasted in a moderate oven (180 deg C, 350 deg F, Gas Mark 4). At this temperature the outside of the joint is sealed, and the flow of juices is reduced during cooking. Allow: 35 minutes per ½kg (30 minutes per 1lb) for small joints; 40 minutes per ½kg (35 minutes per 1lb) for large joints; 45 minutes per ½kg (40 minutes per 1lb) for stuffed joints.

**Accompaniments for roast lamb:** Mint sauce, onion sauce, gravy, and redcurrant jelly.

Carving lamb
1. Loin: *Cut downwards between rib bones. Remove chine bone before carving.*
2. Fillet of leg: *Cut downwards in 6mm (¼in) slices*
3. Best end of neck: *Use method for loin*
4. Shank of leg: *Make cut in centre of leg, carving down to the bone. Continue cutting 6mm (¼in) slices from each side of first cut. Turn joint over, remove any fat, carve horizontal slices along leg. Hold knuckle in napkin to steady joint.*
5. & 6. Shoulder: *5. Hold knuckle in napkin and carve a long slice from centre down. Continue slicing on each side of the first cut. 6. Cut horizontal slices towards knuckle, turning joint where necessary. At knuckle cut downwards.*

## ROSY ROASTED LAMB
*For 6 to 8 portions*

700g (1½lb ) potatoes
25g (1oz) lard
1 (1½kg/3lb) leg of lamb

### Glaze
4×15ml spoons (2 rounded tablespoons) redcurrant jelly
2×15ml spoons (1 rounded tablespoon) thick honey
2×5ml spoons (2 teaspoons) lemon juice
1×15ml spoon (1 level tablespoon) plain flour
Salt and pepper
Sprig of rosemary (optional)

1. Prepare a moderate oven (180 deg C, 350 deg F, Gas Mark 4).
2. Peel potatoes and cut into medium-sized pieces.
3. Melt lard in roasting tin, then coat potatoes in fat.
4. Wipe meat and score the surface of lamb in a diamond pattern, to allow glaze to penetrate.
5. Place meat in roasting tin and cook for 35 minutes.
6. Make glaze: Place redcurrant jelly, honey and lemon juice in a small saucepan over a moderate heat. Stir occasionally, until jelly has melted.
7. Remove meat from oven; brush generously with glaze, baste potatoes with fat from tin
8. Return meat to oven and cook for a further 35 to 50 minutes, brushing occasionally with glaze.
9. Lift meat on to a warmed serving dish; arrange potatoes around lamb and keep warm. Garnish with rosemary.
10. Strain most of fat from roasting tin; stir in flour and 250ml (½ pint) vegetable stock or water and bring to boil, stirring.
11. Taste and season with a little salt and a shake of pepper; pour into a warmed gravy boat.
12. Serve roast lamb with gravy, potatoes and a green vegetable.

*Below: Rosy roasted lamb*

## SPICY ROASTED LOIN OF LAMB
*For 4 to 6 portions*

1kg (2lb) joint loin of lamb
Stuffing
50g (2oz) fresh white breadcrumbs
2×5ml spoons (2 level teaspoons) grated lemon rind
2×5ml spoons (1 rounded teaspoon) ground ginger
1×15ml spoons (1 level tablespoon) soft brown sugar (light)
1 egg
250g (½lb) carrots
1×113g (4oz) pack frozen peas
Salt

1. Ask your butcher to bone the lamb for you.
2. Prepare a moderate oven (180 deg C, 350 deg F, Gas Mark 4).
3. Place breadcrumbs, lemon rind, ginger, sugar and egg in a basin.

Above: *Spicy roasted lamb*

Mix together with a fork, until mixture binds together.

**4.** Place lamb on a board, boned side uppermost and thick end facing towards you. Spread stuffing down centre of lamb, roll up and tie securely with string.

**5.** Place lamb in a small roasting tin, in centre of oven, and cook for 1 to 1½ hours, until meat is tender.

**6.** Meanwhile, peel and thinly slice carrots; cook in boiling, salted water for 8 to 10 minutes, or until tender. Drain and keep warm. Cook peas, as directed on pack; drain and keep warm.

**7.** Place lamb on a warmed serving dish; remove string. Arrange carrots at each corner of dish and peas in between.

**8.** Cut meat into slices and serve with creamed potatoes.

# HARICOT LAMB HOT POT
*For 4 to 6 portions*

---

100g (4oz) dried haricot beans
¾kg (1½lb) middle neck of lamb
25g (1oz) plain flour
1×5ml spoon (1 level teaspoon) mixed dried herbs
1×5ml spoon (1 level teaspoon) salt
Pepper
1 medium-sized onion
250g (½lb) carrots
25g (1oz) margarine
1 large (396g/14oz) can tomatoes
2×5ml spoons (2 level teaspoons) granulated sugar
Chopped parsley

---

**1.** Place beans in a bowl, cover with boiling water and leave for 1½ hours, then drain.

**2.** Prepare a moderate oven (180 deg C, 350 deg F, Gas Mark 4).

**3.** Trim lamb; cut off any excess fat. Place flour, herbs, salt and a shake of pepper on a plate; mix well. Coat lamb in seasoned flour.

**4.** Peel and finely slice onion and carrots.

**5.** Melt margarine in a frying pan; fry meat quickly to brown on all sides; place in a 2 litre (4 pint) casserole.

**6.** Fry onion and carrots gently for 3 to 4 minutes; add to casserole, with beans.

**7.** Stir any remaining seasoned flour into fat in frying pan. Add contents of can of tomatoes, half a can of water and sugar. Bring to boil, stirring, and pour over lamb and vegetables in casserole; cover with a lid.

**8.** Place in centre of oven for 1½ to 1¾ hours, until lamb and vegetables are tender. Taste and season with more salt and pepper, if necessary. Sprinkle with chopped parsley.

**9.** Serve with a green vegetable and creamed potatoes.

Below: *Haricot lamb hot pot*

## MINTY ROLLED SHOULDER

*For 6 to 8 portions*

---

1 1½kg (3lb) shoulder of lamb
6×15ml spoons (6 level
    tablespoons) parsley and thyme
    stuffing mix
3×15ml spoons (3 level
    tablespoons) chopped mint
1×15ml spoon (1 level
    tablespoon) castor sugar
100ml (4 fluid oz) boiling water
6 medium-sized onions
1×15ml spoon (1 level
    tablespoon) plain flour
Salt and pepper

---

**1.** Ask your butcher to bone the lamb for you.
**2.** Prepare a moderate oven (180 deg C, 350 deg F, Gas Mark 4).

**3.** Place stuffing mix, mint, sugar and boiling water in a basin. Mix together with a wooden spoon.
**4.** Press stuffing into bone cavity of joint. Roll up; tie securely with string.
**5.** Place in roasting tin, in centre of oven, and cook for 1 hour.
**6.** Meanwhile, peel onions. After lamb has been cooking for 1 hour, arrange onions around and baste with a little fat. Cook for a further 1 hour, until lamb is cooked and onions are tender.
**7.** Lift meat on to a warmed serving dish and remove string; arrange onions around lamb.
**8.** Strain most of fat from roasting tin; stir in flour and 250 ml (½ pint) vegetable stock or water. Bring to boil, stirring; taste and season with salt and pepper.
**9.** Pour gravy into a warmed gravy

Above: *Minty rolled shoulder*

boat and serve with roast lamb, onions, potatoes and green beans.

12

## NOISETTES OF LAMB WITH MUSHROOM SAUCE

*For 4 to 6 portions*

1 joint best end neck of lamb
1 medium-sized onion
100g ($\frac{1}{4}$lb) button mushrooms
25g (1oz) lard
25g (1oz) plain flour
125ml ($\frac{1}{4}$ pint) dry white wine
   or cider
1 chicken stock cube
1 × 5ml spoon (1 level teaspoon)
   granulated sugar
Salt and pepper
1 head of celery
1 medium-sized tomato

**1.** Ask your butcher to bone the lamb.
**2.** Roll up lamb firmly; tie securely with string at 1cm ($\frac{1}{2}$in) intervals. Cut lamb, in between string, into noisettes.
**3.** Peel and finely chop onion; wash and finely chop mushrooms.
**4.** Melt lard in a frying pan; fry noisettes over a moderate heat for about 15 to 20 minutes, turning occasionally, until lamb is tender.
**5.** Arrange the noisettes on a warmed serving dish; keep warm.
**6.** Fry onion and mushrooms for 2 to 3 minutes, until onion is tender. Stir in flour and cook for 1 minute. Add wine or cider, 250ml ($\frac{1}{2}$ pint) water, chicken stock cube and sugar, bring to boil, stirring, cover and simmer for 30 minutes.
**7.** Taste and season with salt and pepper; pour a little of the sauce over noisettes and place remainder in a warmed sauce boat.

*Above: Noisettes of lamb with mushroom sauce*

**8.** Meanwhile, wash celery; chop finely. Cook in boiling, salted water for 10 to 12 minutes, until tender. Drain and arrange in a border around noisettes.
**9.** Cut tomato into 5 wedges and arrange one wedge at each side of noisettes. Serve with sauté potatoes.

## CARVING BEEF

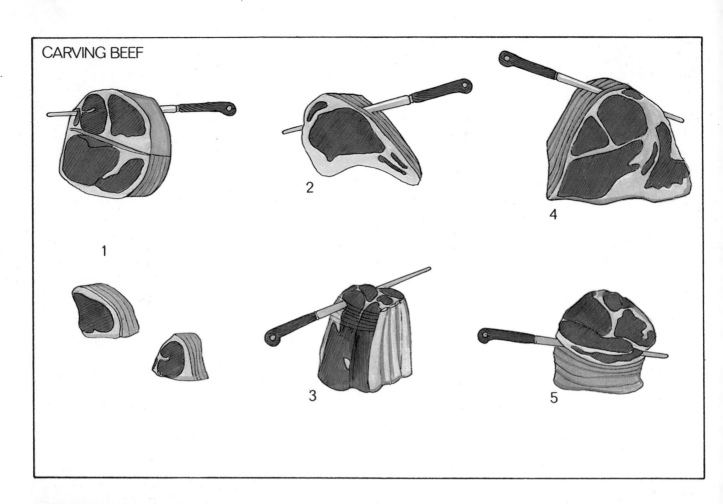

1

2

4

3

5

# Beef

**Look for these points when buying beef:** The redness of beef varies after cutting and exposure to air, but this need not affect your choice. Look for a fresh, slightly moist appearance. The lean part of roasting joints should be smooth and velvety in texture. Coarse lean meat is generally an

**Carving beef**
1. Sirloin: *Carve out the flank part, then fillet as shown; cut them down across grain in thin slices. Turn the joint, with remaining meat on top, and carve downwards to centre bone.*
2. Fore rib: *Place the meat flat on a dish, then cut in slices.*
3. Top rib: *Cut down to the bone in thin slices, removing the skewers only where necessary.*
4. Aitchbone: *Cut in thin slices downwards to the bone and across the grain.*
5. Rolled rib: *Cut across the grain of meat in thin slices.*

Cuts of beef: *1. Aitchbone 2. Fore rib 3. Top rib 4. Wing end of sirloin 5. Fillet end of sirloin. 6. Flank 7. Top rump 8. Brisket 9. Blade bone 10. Top side 11. Back rib 12. Rump 13. Chuck 14. Leg 15. Sticking 16. Skirt 17. Shin 18. Silverside*

indication that meat is suitable only for braising and stewing. Beef that is very coarse will almost certainly be tough.

The lean should be surrounded by a layer of creamy-white fat. The colour may vary, but this will not affect the eating qualities. The important thing is to look for fat that is firm and dry. Marbling or flecks of fat in the meat is an aid to successful cooking; the flecks of fat melt into the lean and help retain the meat's full flavour. Beef cuts that have been pickled ready for boiling will be grey in colour. The colour change is caused by the brine, and the meat will turn an attractive pink during cooking.

**Freezing:** Rapid freezing is most important. Always set the freezer control to the coldest setting and set to fast-freeze several hours beforehand. Allow one cubic foot of freezer space for every 1kg to 1½kg (2lb to 3lb) of meat to be frozen. Beef that is fresh and well packed will keep for up to nine months in a freezer.

**Cooking beef:** Prime joints of beef are particularly juicy when served slightly underdone or 'rare', but this is a matter of personal taste. If you prefer your beef cooked evenly right through, ensure that the oven temperature is not too high. The less tender roasting joints—top rump, back rib, top rib, topside and aitchbone—should be slow-roasted. A covered roasting tin is ideal for cooking these joints.

**For roast beef:** Sirloin and wing rib: oven temperature, moderate (190 deg C, 375 deg F, Gas Mark 5). Thick, boned cut— 30 minutes per ½kg (25 minutes per 1lb); thin cut on the bone— 25 minutes per ½kg (20 minutes per 1lb). Back, top and fore rib: oven temperature, moderate (180 deg C, 350 deg F, Gas Mark 4). Thick cut—25 minutes per ½kg (25 minutes per 1lb); thin cut— 25 minutes per ½kg (20 minutes per 1lb).

**Accompaniments for roast beef:** Yorkshire pudding, mustard and gravy.

**For pot roasted or braised joints of beef:** The joint should be placed in a large saucepan or casserole with some root vegetables. The vegetables help to improve the flavour and also provide additional moisture during cooking. Add very little stock and cover with a well-fitting lid. Cook joints slowly; allow 45 minutes per ½kg (40 minutes per 1lb).

**For stews and casseroles:** Add a stock cube or meat extract cube, when making beef casseroles or stews, for added flavour. Long, slow cooking is essential. Allow 2 to 3 hours depending on the quality of steak, and cook at 170 deg C, 325 deg F, Gas Mark 3.

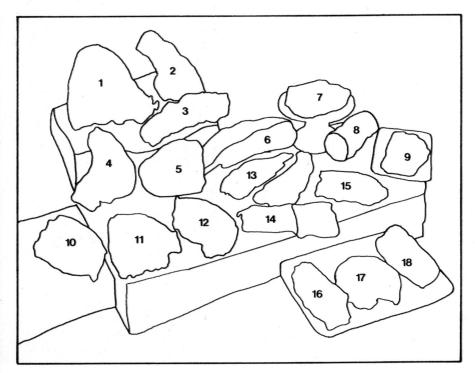

## ROASTED FORE RIB OF BEEF
*For 6 to 8 portions*

25g (1oz) lard
1 (2½kg/5lb) joint fore rib of beef (about 2 bones)
1kg to 1½kg (2lb to 3lb) potatoes
Salt
1 × 15ml spoon (1 level tablespoon) plain flour
Pepper

1. Prepare a moderate oven (180 deg C, 350 deg F, Gas Mark 4).
2. Place lard in a roasting tin and melt in oven.
3. Wipe meat with a piece of moist kitchen paper; place in roasting tin in centre of oven.
4. Peel potatoes; cut into medium-sized pieces. Cook in boiling, salted water for 5 minutes. Drain and arrange potatoes around meat; baste with fat. Cook meat and potatoes for 2 to 2½ hours, basting

## BEEF, TOMATO AND MUSHROOM STEW
*For 4 to 6 portions*

¾kg (1½lb) stewing steak
25g (1oz) plain flour
Salt and pepper
1 medium-sized onion
3 medium-sized leeks
100g (4oz) button mushrooms
50g (2oz) lard
1 large (396g/14oz) can tomatoes

1. Cut meat into 2cm (1in) cubes, removing any excess fat or gristle.
2. Place flour on a plate with 1 × 2·5ml spoon (½ level teaspoon) salt and a shake of pepper. Coat meat in seasoned flour.
3. Peel onion; chop finely. Trim roots, tops and any tough leaves from leeks. Cut leeks halfway through lengthwise, then open out and wash thoroughly, to remove any soil. Cut into rings. Wash mushrooms.
4. Melt 25g (1oz) lard in a large saucepan. Add meat and flour; fry

*Above: Beef, tomato and mushroom stew*

quickly, to brown meat on all sides. Place meat on a plate.
5. Melt remaining lard in saucepan; add onion, leeks and mushrooms. Fry for 4 to 5 minutes; stir in contents of can of tomatoes and a can of water. Bring to boil, stirring; add meat. Cover and cook very gently for 2½ to 2¾ hours, or until meat is tender.
6. Taste and season with more salt and pepper, if necessary. Pour into a warmed serving dish. Serve with jacket or creamed potatoes and a green vegetable.

occasionally with fat.

**5.** Lift meat out on to a warmed serving dish and arrange potatoes around; keep warm.

**6.** Make gravy. Strain most of fat from roasting tin; stir flour and 250ml (½ pint) vegetable stock or water into juices in tin. Bring to boil, stirring. Taste; season with a little salt and a shake of pepper. Pour into a warmed gravy boat.

**7.** Serve roast beef with gravy, roast potatoes, Brussels sprouts, and Yorkshire puddings (see recipe on page 51).

*Note:* Place beef in coolest part of oven for last part of cooking time, while Yorkshire puddings are cooking.

Below: *Roasted fore rib*

## BRAISED STEAK
*For 4 to 6 portions*

¾kg (1½lb) blade bone steak
25g (1oz) plain flour
Salt and pepper
1 small swede
1 medium-sized turnip
1 medium-sized parsnip
1 medium-sized onion
4 sticks of celery
50g (2oz) lard
1 beef stock cube
Chopped parsley

**1.** Prepare a cool oven (170 deg C, 325 deg F, Gas Mark 3).

**2.** Cut steak into portion-sized pieces. Place flour, 2·5ml (½ level teaspoon) salt and a shake of pepper on a plate. Coat meat in seasoned flour.

**3.** Peel swede, turnip, parsnip and onion; cut into even-sized pieces. Scrub celery; cut into slices.

**4.** Melt 25g (1oz) lard in a frying pan, add vegetables; fry lightly until browned. Place in a shallow,

Above: *Braised steak*

2 litre (4 pint) casserole.

**5.** Melt remaining 25g (1oz) lard in frying pan, add meat and fry quickly on all sides to brown. Arrange meat on top of vegetables. Stir any remaining flour into fat remaining in pan.

**6.** Crumble stock cube into pan; stir in 250ml (½ pint) water. Bring to boil, stirring; pour over meat and vegetables.

**7.** Cover with a lid or foil and cook in centre of oven for 1¾ to 2 hours, or until meat is tender.

**8.** Taste and season with more salt and pepper, if necessary. Sprinkle with chopped parsley; serve with creamed potato and peas.

17

## BOILED BEEF AND PEASE PUDDING

*For 5 to 6 portions*

1½ to 1¾kg (3 to 3½lb) joint
   boned and rolled
   salt brisket of beef
5 small onions
6 small carrots

**Pease pudding**
200g (½lb) yellow split peas
1 small onion
25g (1oz) butter
1 × 2·5ml spoon (½ level teaspoon)
   salt
Pepper

**Dumplings**
100g (4oz) self-raising flour
1 × 2·5ml spoon (½ level teaspoon)
   salt
50g (1½oz) shredded suet
Cold water to mix
Chopped parsley

1. Place peas in a basin; cover with cold water. Leave overnight; drain.
2. Wash meat in cold water; place in a large saucepan, cover with cold water and bring to boil slowly. Cover tightly with lid and simmer for 1 hour.
3. Peel 6 onions and carrots. Place 1 onion in a medium-sized saucepan; add drained peas and 570ml (1 pint) water. Bring to boil;cover and simmer for 1 hour or until peas are tender.
4. Add carrots and remaining onions to meat in saucepan; cook meat for a further 1 to 1¼ hours until meat is tender.
5. Remove onion from peas; keep warm to serve with other vegetables. Drain peas in a sieve; rinse saucepan. Press peas through sieve into saucepan; add butter, salt and a shake of pepper and mix well. Alternatively, place peas, butter, salt and a shake of pepper in a liquidiser goblet and blend until smooth; return to saucepan.
6. Place flour and salt in a bowl, stir in suet and add sufficient water,

Above: *Boiled beef and pease pudding*

about 4 × 15ml spoons (3 to 4 tablespoons), to make a soft, but not sticky, dough.
7 Turn out dough on to a floured board and knead lightly. Divide into 6 pieces; lightly shape each piece into a ball.
8. Remove meat and vegetables from saucepan; place on separate warmed serving dishes and keep warm. Pour some of the beef liquor into a warmed gravy boat, leaving about 4cm (1½in) depth of liquor in pan; keep gravy boat warm. Place pan containing liquor on a high heat, add dumplings, cover, lower heat and cook for 15 minutes. Remove dumplings from pan, arrange around meat and sprinkle with chopped parsley.
9. Reheat pease pudding, stirring continuously; then place in warmed serving dish.

## POT-ROASTED BRISKET
*For 6 portions*

2 medium-sized onions
250g (½lb) carrots
4 sticks of celery
100g (4oz) streaky bacon
25g (1oz) lard
1 (1½kg/3lb) joint boned and
 rolled brisket of beef
25ml (½ pint) brown ale
Salt and pepper
1×15ml spoon (1 level tablespoon)
 cornflour

1. Peel onions and carrots; chop onions finely.

2. Wash celery; chop finely. Remove rind and bone from bacon; cut bacon into small pieces.

3. Melt lard in a large saucepan. Add brisket and fry quickly, to brown on all sides. Lift meat out on to a plate.

4. Place onions, carrots, celery and bacon in pan. Fry for 3 to 4 minutes, without browning. Add brown ale, a little salt and a shake of pepper. Bring to boil, return meat to saucepan, cover and cook very gently for 2 to 2½ hours, until meat is tender.

5. Remove brisket from saucepan and place on a warmed serving dish. Arrange carrots around brisket.

6. Blend cornflour with 1 × 15ml spoon (1 tablespoon) water; stir into saucepan. Bring to boil, stirring, and cook for 2 minutes. Taste and season with more salt and pepper, if necessary.

7. Pour some of the gravy and vegetables over the meat; pour remainder into a gravy boat. Serve with boiled potatoes and Brussels sprouts.

*Below: Pot-roasted brisket*

# Pork

## CARVING PORK

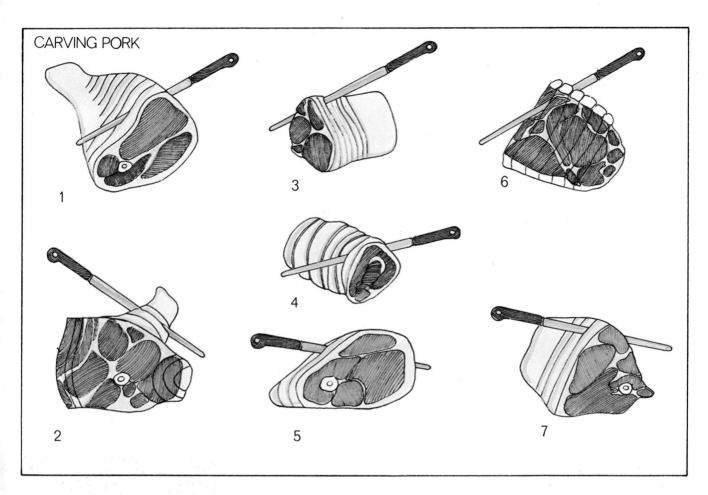

1

3

6

4

2

5

7

Cuts of pork: *1. End loin 2. Middle loin 3. Chops 4. Fillet end leg 5. Knuckle end leg 6. Spare rib 7. Hand and spring 8. Chump end of loin 9. Thick end belly 10. Thin end belly 11. Blade bone*

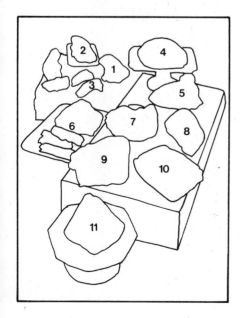

Pork is always available and, with modern refrigeration, there's no need to heed the old wives' tale that it is only safe to eat pork when there's an 'r' in the month. Every joint of pork can be roasted, and individual cuts are suitable for grilling and frying. The economical cuts, shoulder, hand and spring and belly, can also be used to make casseroles, stews and pies.

Pork is equally good served hot or cold and it's a meat that lends itself to being served in a variety of different ways when cold: sausages, both fresh and smoked, brawn, bacon, black pudding and pâtés.

Lard is rendered from pork fat. Pork can be pickled in a brine and saltpetre solution, or salted and cured to make bacon.

**Look for these points when buying pork:** Look for finely-

Carving pork
1. Leg: *Cut 6mm ( $\frac{1}{4}$ in) slices through the crackling, down to the bone.*
2. Hand and spring: *Carve from either side of bone across the grain of the meat, then down to the bone.*
3. Loin: *Cut downwards and through rib bones, as shown.*
4. Middle cut rolled belly: *Cut 6mm ( $\frac{1}{4}$ in) slices through the crackling and down through the meat.*
5. Fillet of leg: *Cut downwards in 6mm ( $\frac{1}{4}$ in) slices to the bone.*
6. Spare ribs: *Cut down between the bones into chops.*
7. Blade: *Slice through crackling down to the bone. Slices will be shorter in the centre, where the bone humps. Turn joint over and cut at an oblique angle to get the longest slices.*

grained, pinkish flesh. The fat should be firm and creamy white. Stale pork is brownish in colour and the fat is soft and grey.

**Freezing:** Pork that is fresh and

21

well packed will keep for up to six months in the freezer.

**Cooking pork:** To roast pork: weigh joint and place in roasting tin. Score skin finely. Brush skin with oil or melted fat; sprinkle liberally with salt and rub salt into the cuts. This gives a crisp crackling. Place rolled joints on a rack in roasting tin. For roast pork: Joints up to 2½kg (5lb): oven temperature, moderate (190 deg C, 375 deg F, Gas Mark 5), 35 minutes per ½kg plus 35 minutes (30 minutes per 1lb plus 30 minutes). Large joints: oven temperature, moderate (180 deg C, 350 deg F, Gas Mark 4), 40 minutes per ½kg plus 40 minutes (35 minutes per 1lb plus 35 minutes).

Thin joints will cook more quickly than boned and rolled joints.

**Accompaniments for roast pork:** Sage and onion stuffing, sausagemeat stuffing, apple sauce or fried apples, prunes and cranberry sauce.

## ROAST LEG OF PORK WITH SAGE AND ONION APPLES
*For 8 to 10 portions*

3kg (6lb) knuckle end of leg of pork
Oil
Salt
1kg (2lb) potatoes

**Stuffing**
1 medium-sized onion
1×15ml spoon (1 tablespoon) oil
1 egg
1×15ml spoon (1 tablespoon) milk
100g (4oz) fresh white breadcrumbs
1×5ml spoon (1 level teaspoon) dried sage
1×2·5ml spoon (½ level teaspoon) salt
Pepper
3 small cooking apples

1. Prepare a moderate oven (180 deg C, 350 deg F, Gas Mark 4).
2. Score skin of pork with a sharp knife. Brush skin with oil and sprinkle liberally with salt; rub salt into cuts in meat.
3. Place meat in a roasting tin and cook in centre of oven for about 4 hours, until meat is tender and crackling crisp.
4. Wash and peel potatoes; cut into even-sized pieces. Cook in boiling, salted water for 3 minutes; drain and place in roasting tin 1½ hours before end of cooking time.

5. Make stuffing: Peel and chop onion. Heat oil in a medium-sized saucepan; add onion and cook for 3 to 4 minutes, until onion is soft, but not browned. Remove from heat. Beat egg and milk together in a small basin. Stir milk mixture, breadcrumbs, sage, salt and a shake of pepper into saucepan; mix well.
6. Core apples and cut in halves. Pile a little stuffing on each apple and place in a small tin. Cook just below centre of oven for 40 minutes, until apples are cooked.
7. Place pork and stuffed apples on a warmed serving dish and roast potatoes in another warmed dish. Drain off fat from roasting tin and use drippings to make gravy. Serve with a green vegetable.

## BLADE OF PORK WITH VEGETABLES
*For 4 portions*

1½kg (3lb) blade of pork
2 medium-sized onions
1 large carrot
½kg (1lb) potatoes
25g (1oz) margarine
2×15ml spoons (2 level tablespoons) plain flour
1 large (396g/14oz) can tomatoes
1×5ml spoon (1 level teaspoon) salt
1×5ml spoon (1 level teaspoon) sugar
1×2·5ml spoon (½ level teaspoon) mixed dried herbs
Pepper

1. Bone blade of pork or ask your butcher to do this for you.
2. Prepare a moderate oven (180 deg C, 350 deg F, Gas Mark 4).
3. Remove rind and excess fat from meat. Roll up meat and tie with string.
4. Peel and slice onions and carrot. Wash and peel potatoes; cut in halves, if large.

**5.** Melt margarine in a large saucepan; add pork and fry quickly on all sides. Remove meat and place in a 2 litre (4 pint) casserole. Add onions and carrot to fat remaining in saucepan and fry for 3 to 4 minutes, until onions are soft, but not browned. Stir in flour, contents of can of tomatoes, 125ml ($\frac{1}{4}$ pint) water, salt, sugar, mixed dried herbs and a shake of pepper. Bring to boil, stirring; add potatoes and place tomato mixture in casserole, with meat. Cover casserole and cook in centre of oven for $1\frac{1}{2}$ to $1\frac{3}{4}$ hours until meat is tender.

**6.** Place pork on a warmed serving dish; remove string and place vegetables around meat. Pour over a little sauce and serve remainder in a warmed sauce boat. Serve with green beans.

Below: *Blade of pork with vegetables*

## PORK CHOPS WITH SAVOURY POTATO

*For 4 portions*

4 spare rib pork chops
Salt and pepper
$\frac{3}{4}$kg (1$\frac{1}{2}$lb) potatoes
1 medium-sized onion
2 tomatoes
Knob of butter
Milk
Watercress to garnish

**1.** Prepare a moderate grill; remove grill rack. Trim any excess fat from chops. Place chops in grill pan; sprinkle with a little salt and pepper. Grill chops for 20 to 25 minutes, turning once.

**2.** Wash and peel potatoes; cut into even-sized pieces. Cook in boiling, salted water for 20 minutes, until tender.

**3.** Peel and slice onion. Place in

Above: *Pork chops with savoury potato*

grill pan with chops; cook for 10 minutes, turning occasionally. Cut tomatoes in halves and sprinkle with a little salt and pepper. Place in grill pan; cook for 4 minutes.

**4.** Drain potatoes, dry over a low heat, then mash with a fork or potato masher. Add a knob of butter, a little milk, salt and pepper; beat together with a wooden spoon. Stir in onion.

**5.** Pile potato mixture on a warmed serving dish. Arrange chops on top of potato, and halved tomatoes at either end of dish. Use drippings in grill pan to make gravy. Garnish with sprigs of watercress.

23

## WILTSHIRE PORK WITH RICE
*For 4 portions*

2×15ml spoons (2 level tablespoons) plain flour

Salt and pepper

¾kg (1½lb) pie pork

2 medium-sized onions

100g (¼lb) button mushrooms

1×15ml spoon (1 tablespoon) oil

250ml (½ pint) sweet cider

1 chicken extract cube

2×15ml spoons (2 level tablespoons) tomato purée

200g (8oz) long-grain rice

1. Mix flour, 1×5ml (1 level teaspoon) salt and a shake of pepper together on a plate. Coat meat in seasoned flour.

2. Peel and slice onions. Wash mushrooms. Heat oil in a medium-sized saucepan. Add onions and meat and fry for 3 minutes, stirring occasionally. Stir in any remaining seasoned flour, cider, extract cube, mushrooms and tomato purée. Bring to boil, cover and simmer for 30 minutes.

3. Cook rice in boiling, salted water for 12 minutes. Test by pressing a grain between thumb and finger; drain in a sieve and rinse with hot water.

4. Arrange rice at each end of a warmed serving dish. Taste and add more salt and pepper to pork, if necessary. Place pork mixture between rice and serve with peas.

## SWEET AND SOUR LOIN OF PORK
*For 4 portions*

1kg (2½lb) loin of pork

1 (340g/12oz) can pineapple cubes

1 small onion

1 small green pepper

1×15ml spoon (1 tablespoon) oil

2×15ml spoons (2 level tablespoons) brown sugar

1×10ml spoon (2 teaspoons) Worcestershire sauce

2×15ml spoons (2 level tablespoons) tomato ketchup

1×15ml spoon (1 level tablespoon) tomato chutney

1×2·5ml spoon (½ level teaspoon) salt

1×15ml spoon (1 level tablespoon) cornflour

2×15ml spoons (2 tablespoons) malt vinegar

1. Ask your butcher to chine meat and remove skin. Prepare a moderate oven (190 deg C, 375 deg F, Gas Mark 5).

2. Place pork in a small roasting tin. Drain pineapple and pour syrup over pork. Roast pork in centre of oven for 1¾ hours, basting occasionally.

3. Meanwhile, prepare sauce. Peel and chop onion. Cut pepper in half lengthwise; discard seeds, core and white pith. Slice pepper.

4. Heat oil in a medium-sized saucepan. Add onion and cook for 3 to 4 minutes, until onion is soft, but not browned. Stir in sliced pepper, sugar, Worcestershire sauce, tomato ketchup, tomato chutney, 125ml (¼ pint) water and salt. Blend cornflour with vinegar and add to saucepan.

5. Bring to boil, stirring; cover. Simmer for 15 minutes. Halve pineapple cubes; add to sauce. Heat for 1 minute.

6. Place joint on a warmed serving plate; place sauce around pork and serve with boiled rice and peas.

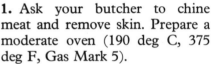

Left: *Sweet and sour pork*

# Bacon

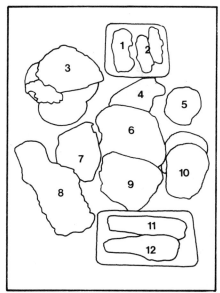

Cuts of bacon: *1. Oyster rashers 2. Streaky rashers 3. Collar joint 4. Gammon knuckle 5. Vacuum-packed gammon joint 6. Middle gammon 7. Gammon slipper 8. Rolled and boned forehock 9. Corner gammon 10. Gammon*

Bacon is much more than a breakfast food. Rashers and joints can be cooked by various methods and served for meals at any time of the day, and bacon is available throughout the year.

Bacon is the cured meat from the sides and back of a pig that is bred especially for its high proportion of lean to fat. When bacon is preserved in salt it is called 'green bacon', recognisable by its pale rind and pink flesh. Smoked bacon is green bacon which has been hung above smouldering sawdust for about two days, producing a golden brown rind and a darker pink flesh. A ham is the prime leg joint of a pig.

**Look for these points when buying bacon:** Good-quality, correctly cured bacon should have a pleasant smell with no stickiness. The rind should be thin and smooth, the fat firm and free from any yellow marks. The lean should be a good deep pink, adhering closely to the bone. It's easier to buy ready-prepared joints — boned and rolled as required— and rashers sliced to the required thickness. You can buy bacon fresh-cut, film-wrapped and vacuum-packed; some of the vacuum-packed joints may be boiled in the bag.

**Freezing:** As bacon is a cured meat it will not keep as well as fresh meat once it is frozen. Only freeze fresh bacon joints cut into the required serving size and rashers in usable amounts as it is unwise to re-freeze bacon once it has been thawed. Bacon will keep for the following times: vacuum-packed rashers and joints—up to ten weeks; fresh-cut smoked bacon joints—up to eight weeks; fresh-cut unsmoked bacon—up to five weeks; fresh-cut rashers, steaks and chops—up to four weeks. Smoked bacon always keeps for twice as long as green bacon, because of the smoking process.

## Cooking Bacon

**Soaking:** A three-hour soaking is sufficient before cooking, especially now that mild cured bacon with a reduced salt content is more readily available. When time is short, soaking can be entirely eliminated by bringing the bacon to the boil and replacing with fresh water.

**Roasting:** Allow 30 minutes per ½kg plus 30 minutes (25 minutes per 1lb plus 25 minutes). Place soaked joint in a saucepan, cover with cold water, bring to boil and cook for half the calculated time. Remove from pan, strip off skin, place in a roasting tin and cook in a moderate oven (190 deg C, 375 deg F, Gas Mark 5) for the remaining time. Gammon joints need not be parboiled; just soak, then place in a roasting tin and wrap in foil. After half the cooking time, open foil and strip off skin, glaze if desired, then cook uncovered for the remaining time.

**Baking:** As for roasting, but wrap joint in foil for the second half of cooking time.

**Braising:** Allow 40 minutes per ½kg plus 40 minutes (35 minutes per 1lb plus 35 minutes). Parboil soaked joint for half the cooking time—see roasting—then remove skin and place joint in a casserole with some lightly fried vegetables. Add a little stock, cover and cook in a moderate oven (180 deg C, 350 deg F, Gas Mark 4) for the remaining time. If desired, remove lid for the last 30 minutes to allow joint to brown. Alternatively place soaked joint in a casserole and cook for full time; remove lid if desired to brown joint.

**Frying and grilling:** Remove rind if desired, snip fat of steaks and chops to prevent curling and uneven cooking. Lay rashers, overlapping, in frying pan or on grill rack, fat side underneath for frying, on top for grilling.

**Pressure cooking:** Place soaked bacon on trivet in pressure cooker, add 250ml (½ pint) water, bring pressure cooker up to high (15lb) pressure and cook for one-third of normal boiling time. Alterna-

tively, if you haven't time to soak bacon, remove trivet, place unsoaked joint in pressure cooker, cover with water, bring to boil, remove bacon and drain. Then proceed to cook as above.

## COLD CUT COLLAR
*For 6 portions*

---

1kg (2½lb) joint collar bacon
2 medium-sized carrots
1 medium-sized onion
6 peppercorns
2 bay leaves
1 × 15ml spoon (1 level tablespoon) brown sugar
Browned breadcrumbs

---

1. Place bacon in a bowl, cover with cold water and leave to soak for at least 3 hours. Drain and place joint in a saucepan; cover with water. Bring to boil, remove from heat and drain.
2. Meanwhile peel and cut carrots into 2cm (1in) pieces. Peel onion and cut into quarters. Cover joint with fresh water, add carrots, onion, peppercorns, bay leaves and sugar. Bring to boil, cover and simmer, allowing 25 minutes per ½kg plus 25 minutes (20 minutes per 1lb plus 20 minutes).
3. Remove joint from saucepan, leave until completely cold. Remove string and rind from bacon. Place breadcrumbs on a sheet of greaseproof paper. Press fat of bacon into breadcrumbs. Serve with a crisp green salad.

Top: *Cold cut collar*

Centre: *West country bacon braise*

Right: *Gammon grill with glazed apples*

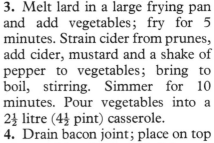

## WEST COUNTRY BACON BRAISE
*For about 8 portions*

100g (4oz) prunes
375ml ($\frac{3}{4}$ pint) dry cider
1kg (2$\frac{1}{2}$lb) joint of forehock bacon
3 medium-sized carrots
250g ($\frac{1}{2}$lb) onions
250g ($\frac{1}{2}$lb) swede
4 sticks of celery
25g (1oz) lard
1 × 2·5ml spoon ($\frac{1}{2}$ level teaspoon) dry mustard
Pepper
1$\frac{1}{2}$ × 15ml spoons (1$\frac{1}{2}$ level tablespoons) cornflour
Gravy browning

1. Place prunes in a basin, cover with cider and leave overnight. Place bacon in a bowl, cover with cold water and leave to soak for at least 3 hours.
2. Prepare a moderately hot oven (200 deg C, 400 deg F, Gas Mark 6). Peel carrots and cut into 2cm (1in) pieces. Peel onions; cut into quarters. Peel swede; cut into chunks. Wash celery; cut into 2cm (1in) pieces.
3. Melt lard in a large frying pan and add vegetables; fry for 5 minutes. Strain cider from prunes, add cider, mustard and a shake of pepper to vegetables; bring to boil, stirring. Simmer for 10 minutes. Pour vegetables into a 2$\frac{1}{2}$ litre (4$\frac{1}{2}$ pint) casserole.
4. Drain bacon joint; place on top of vegetables. Cover with lid; cook in centre of oven for 1 hour.
5. Remove string and skin from joint; add prunes to casserole and return to centre of oven without lid for a further 20 to 40 minutes, depending on thickness of joint.
6. Place bacon and vegetables on a warmed serving dish; keep warm. Blend cornflour and a few drops gravy browning with 1 × 15ml spoon (1 tablespoon) water. Stir gravy into casserole; return casserole to oven for 5 minutes.
7. Strain thickened gravy into a gravy boat. Serve with jacket potatoes, which may be cooked in oven on same shelf as meat, and peas.

*Note:* Any remaining bacon can be served cold.

## GAMMON GRILL WITH GLAZED APPLES
*For 4 portions*

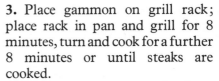

4 thick gammon steaks (about 1kg/1$\frac{3}{4}$lb)
1 medium-sized cooking apple
4 medium-sized tomatoes
Oil
1 × 15ml spoon (1 level tablespoon) thick-cut marmalade
1 × 5 ml (1 level teaspoon) dried oregano or marjoram (optional)
1 packet potato sticks
Watercress

1. Remove rack from grill pan and prepare a medium grill. Remove rind from gammon and snip fat at regular intervals to prevent curling.
2. Peel and core apple; slice into 4 rings. Cut a cross on top of each tomato. Place rings and tomatoes in grill pan; brush with oil.
3. Place gammon on grill rack; place rack in pan and grill for 8 minutes, turn and cook for a further 8 minutes or until steaks are cooked.
4. Remove gammon steaks from grill rack: place on a serving plate and keep warm. Turn apple slices, place on grill rack and brush with marmalade. Place tomatoes on rack and sprinkle with oregano or marjoram if desired.
5. Return to grill until tomatoes and apple slices are cooked.
6. To serve: Arrange tomatoes, apple slices and potato sticks on serving plate around gammon steaks. Garnish with watercress. Cut gammon steaks in halves to serve.

# Offal

Offal and fancy meats are the names given to various internal organs, like liver, kidney and heart, and external parts, such as oxtail, of an animal carcass. You will find each has its own quite distinctive flavour and texture.

**Look for these points when buying:** Good-quality, fresh offal should have no spots or unfamiliar marks and no unpleasant smell. The texture should be firm. Liver, brains, kidney, tripe and heart should be bought the day they are required, but pig's head, trotters, oxtail and tongue will store in the refrigerator for up to four days. Some cuts of offal such as sweetbreads, kidney, liver and heart are available frozen, and should be carefully thawed, but never re-frozen.

**Freezing:** Only freeze fresh offal. Raw offal will store for up to two months in a freezer; thaw at room temperature and use immediately.

*Offal: 1. Ox tongue 2. Pig's head 3. Plain and honeycomb tripe 4. Pig's, lamb's, calf's and ox liver 5. Chicken livers 6. Ox tail 7. Calf's kidneys 8. Lamb's kidneys 9. Ox kidney 10. Calf's brain 11. Lambs' brains 12. Calf's foot 13. Pig's trotters 14. Lambs' hearts 15. Ox heart 16. Calves' sweetbreads 17. Lambs' sweetbreads 18. Calf's tongue 19. Lambs' tongues*

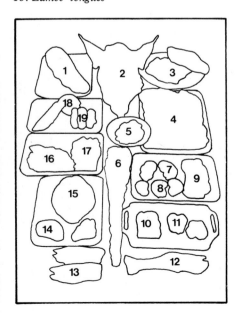

## Cuts of Offal

**Kidney:** Kidney is one of the most popular types of offal. The kidneys of many animals are available: ox, calves', lambs' and pigs' are the most popular. All kidneys are highly nutritious, containing good proportions of protein and iron. Ox kidney and calves' kidneys are multi-lobed and the largest; lambs' and pigs' are smaller and have the distinctive 'kidney' shape. Lambs' kidneys may still be bought in a covering of suet, while pigs' kidneys are often cut with pork chops. Ox and pigs' kidneys are the strongest in flavour, ox kidney being very well suited to the distinctive flavour of steak and kidney pudding. Calves' and lambs' kidneys have a more delicate flavour and may be quickly cooked in grills, kebabs or in rich sauces. To prepare, remove any membrane surrounding the kidneys. For ox and calves' kidneys, the lobes should be removed with scissors; pigs' and lambs' kidneys need to be cut through to the centre and their cores removed.

**Liver:** Calves', ox, pigs', lambs' and poultry livers are of outstanding nutritional value, rich in protein, vitamin A, the B complex, and iron. Calf's liver is the best quality; it has a mild flavour and is quick to cook by frying or grilling. Ox liver is much cheaper, has a coarser texture, and needs long, slow cooking to tenderise. Lamb's liver is mild; it is usually fried and served with bacon. Pig's liver is strong, relatively inexpensive and is best used in pâtés and for sausage-making. Chicken livers are rich and inexpensive; use for pâtés and galantines, or serve grilled or fried on toast as an after-dinner savoury.

**Oxtail** should have an even amount of brightly coloured meat to bone, with creamy white fat. One oxtail is usually enough for four portions and is best bought jointed. For maximum flavour, oxtail needs long, slow cooking, though it may be pressure cooked. Use for meaty soups and stews.

**Tongue:** You can buy tongues of ox, calves and lambs. Ox tongue is the most familiar. It is available canned, or cooked and sliced. Ox tongues weigh about 1½kg to 2kg (3lb to 4lb), and can be bought fresh, brined or smoked. Tongue is principally a protein food. It is very economical and may easily be cooked at home by boiling or pressure cooking, then boning, skinning and pressing. Calves' tongues weigh about ½kg to 1kg (1lb to 2lb) each. They are a bit more delicate in flavour and texture than ox tongue. They may be served with a savoury sauce. Lambs' tongues are the smallest, weighing about 200g to 300g (8oz to 12oz) each. After pre-cooking and skinning, they may be served hot with traditional Cumberland sauce or chopped and added to a white sauce for a tasty vol-au-vent filling.

**Heart:** Lambs' hearts are easily recognisable by their shape. They weigh about 150g to 200g (6oz to 8oz) each and serve one portion each. Ox hearts are the largest, weighing about 1kg (2lb) each. They're usually sold sliced. Hearts should look fresh, with bright reddish meat and creamy fat. To prepare lambs' hearts, wash thoroughly in cold water. Cut off flaps, lobes and gristle found at the top and inside of hearts. Remove membrane dividing the cavities and soak hearts for at least 30 minutes. As heart meat is dense, it requires long, slow cooking, so it is best suited to stewing or braising. alternatively, lambs' hearts can be stuffed and then roasted.

**Sweetbreads** are one of the most expensive and delicate types of offal. Ox, lambs' and calves' sweetbreads are all available. Sweetbreads from the heart region are in two oval parts, while the throat sweetbreads are of a less regular shape, and more elongated. The flesh of both types is white and very soft. They are both extremely nutritious, containing a very high proportion of protein. The most delicate and expensive sweetbreads are lambs'. Ox sweetbreads are cheaper, quite a lot coarser and need long, slow cooking. Calves' sweetbreads strike a happy medium, being inexpensive and tender. To prepare sweetbreads thoroughly wash then soak in salted water for several hours; change the water when it becomes discoloured. Drain, cover with cold water, bring to boil and simmer for 15 to 20 minutes, until tender. Drain, leave covered with cold water until they are cool enough to handle, then remove any skin or fat. Place sweetbreads between two plates and press down with a 1kg (2lb) weight or bag of sugar. They can then be stored for up to two days in the refrigerator, or cooked in various ways by braising, frying in butter, or served in a sauce with other ingredients.

**Feet:** Pigs' trotters, calves' feet and cowheel are sold. Pigs' trotters are the most popular; they are very cheap, costing only a few pence each. They are very gelatinous when cooked, which makes them ideal ingredients for brawn, savoury jellies and meat loaves. They require long, slow cooking. Calves' feet are used in similar ways to pigs' trotters and in particular for calf's foot jelly, a traditional 'light' food for convalescents. Cowheel is large and needs chopping before cooking. It makes good foundation stock

for stews, soups and savoury jellies.

**Heads:** Pigs', calves' and sheeps' heads contain a large amount of meat, tongue, cheek and brains, which are especially good for pies, brawn and soups. Pig's cheek is sometimes boned, brined and boiled and sold as Bath Chap; it is served cold with salads. Ox cheek has a good proportion of meat. It requires long, slow cooking and is best suited to stews and braises. Boar's head, the traditional centre-piece for festive occasions, is very economical for large-scale catering. The head is stuffed and the skin glazed; an apple in the boar's mouth completes the dish.

**Brains:** Calves' brains are the best quality although lambs' and pigs' brains are very popular as there is very little difference in flavour. Brains are sold in sets, but allow approximately 100g (4oz) per portion when buying. They are extremely perishable and delicate and need care when washing. To cook brains, soak in salted water for 15 to 20 minutes. Place in a saucepan, cover with water and add 1 × 10ml spoon (1 rounded teaspoon) salt and 1 × 15ml spoon (1 tablespoon) vinegar or lemon juice to each ½ litre (1 pint) of water. Bring to the boil, cover and simmer for 15 minutes, drain and serve with a savoury sauce, or coat in breadcrumbs and fry.

**Tripe:** Tripe is part of the stomach lining of a cow. It is available in two varieties; plain, from the first stomach, and honeycomb from the second lining. Tripe is a pale cream in colour and is sold in sheets, about 6mm to 1·3cm (¼in to ½in) thick, with the texture of a firm jelly. Fresh tripe is usually sold partially cooked and blanched by the butcher. It is very nutritious, containing more calcium than any other meat. It is light and easy to digest, and is therefore a useful food for convalescents. If bought uncooked, double the cooking time.

## SWEET AND SOUR LAMBS' TONGUES
*For 4 portions*

1 stick celery
1 small onion
½kg (1lb) lambs' tongues
1 × 5ml spoon (1 level teaspoon) salt
Pepper
200g (8oz) long grain rice

### Sauce
1 medium-sized onion
1 small green pepper
Margarine
2 × 15ml spoons (3 rounded teaspoons) cornflour
2 × 15ml spoons (2 level tablespoons) tomato chutney
3 × 15ml spoons (3 level tablespoons) tomato purée
1 × 10ml spoon (2 teaspoons) soy sauce
1 × 15ml spoon (1 tablespoon) vinegar
1 × 10ml spoon (2 level teaspoons) castor sugar
1 beef extract cube

**1.** Wash and slice celery. Peel and slice onion. Wash lambs' tongues in cold, salted water and place in a medium-sized saucepan. Cover with cold water. Add salt, a shake of pepper, celery and

onion. Bring to boil, cover and simmer for 2 to 2½ hours, until tender. Or cook in a pressure cooker at high (15lb) pressure for 20 minutes. Discard celery and onion. Reserve 250ml (½ pint) stock. Place tongues on a board. Remove skin, gristle and bones and cut tongues into small pieces.

**2.** Cook rice in a large saucepan of boiling, salted water for about 12 minutes. Test by pressing a grain between thumb and finger. Drain in a sieve or colander and rinse with hot water. Place rice on a warmed serving dish and keep warm.

**3.** Make sauce: Peel and slice onion. Cut pepper in half lengthwise; discard seeds, core, and white pith; slice thinly. Heat a knob of margarine in a medium-sized saucepan, add onion; fry for 3 to 4 minutes without browning. stir in cornflour, chutney, tomato purée, soy sauce, vinegar, sugar, green pepper and reserved stock. Crumble extract cube and add to pan. Bring to boil, stirring. Cover and simmer for 10 minutes. Add tongue slices and continue cooking for a further 5 minutes. Serve with rice.

Below: *Sweet and sour lambs' tongues*

## SOMERSET OXTAIL BRAISE
*For 4 portions*

---

2 × 15ml spoons (1 rounded tablespoon) plain flour
1 × 5ml spoon (1 level teaspoon) salt
Pepper
1 oxtail, cut into joints
250g (½lb) carrots
250g (½lb) onions
4 sticks celery
25g (1oz) dripping or lard
375ml (¾ pint) dry cider
1 × 2·5ml spoon (½ level teaspoon) mixed dried herbs
2 beef extract cubes
Parsley

---

**1.** Mix flour, salt and a shake of pepper together on a plate. Coat oxtail in seasoned flour. Peel and slice carrots and onions. Wash and cut celery into small pieces. Prepare a cool oven (150 deg C, 300 deg F, Gas Mark 2).

**2.** Melt dripping or lard in a large saucepan, add oxtail, carrots, onions and celery; fry for 10 to 15 minutes, stirring occasionally. Stir in any remaining flour, cider, 125ml (¼ pint) water and mixed dried herbs. Crumble beef extract cubes into pan, bring to boil.

**3.** Transfer contents of saucepan to a 2 litre (4 pint) casserole. Cover; cook in centre of oven for 3 to 3½ hours, until oxtail is tender. Taste; add more seasoning if necessary. Snip parsley over top. Serve with mashed potato, and a green vegetable.

*Note :* Alternatively, omit 125ml (¼ pint) water and cook in a pressure cooker at high (15lb) pressure, for 45 minutes. Somerset Oxtail Braise may be packed into a rigid container and stored in a freezer for up to 2 months.

## TRIPE AND ONIONS
*For 4 portions*

---

½kg (1lb) tripe
½kg (1lb) onions
25g (1oz) margarine
25g (1oz) plain flour
Milk
1 × 10ml spoon (1 rounded teaspoon) salt
Pepper
½ × 2·5ml spoon (¼ level teaspoon) ground nutmeg
Parsley

---

**1.** Wash tripe well. Cut into 2cm (1in) squares. Peel onions; cut into quarters, then each quarter into halves.

**2.** Place tripe in a small saucepan; add 250ml (½ pint) water, bring to boil, cover and simmer for 2 hours, until tender.

**3.** Melt margarine in a medium-sized saucepan; add onions, cover and cook over a low heat for 10 to 15 minutes, until soft. Stir in flour and cook, stirring continuously, for 2 minutes.

**4.** Drain tripe, reserving 125ml (¼ pint) stock in a measuring jug. Make up to 250ml (½ pint) with milk. Add to onions with salt, a good shake of pepper and nutmeg. Bring to boil, stirring; add tripe and cook for 5 minutes.

**5.** Pour into serving dish. Snip some parsley over the top.

# Poultry

## Look for these points when buying poultry

**Chicken:** A fresh chicken should have an unbroken, straight, pliable breast bone and a plump breast. Hen birds are usually the most expensive because they have a higher proportion of flesh to bone than cock birds. Allow approximately 200g (8oz) raw chicken, including bone, per portion. With stuffing and trimmings a 1½kg (3lb) bird will serve five to six portions.

**Turkey:** A fresh turkey should have bright eyes, white flesh, smooth black legs and a pliable breast bone. A turkey can weigh from 3kg to 12kg (6lb to 25lb) and serve from eight portions upwards. Allow approximately 300g (12oz) raw turkey, including bone, per portion. Hen birds have a higher proportion of flesh to bone.

**Goose:** The breast should be

*Poultry: 1. Turkey 2. Boned and rolled turkey joints 3. Turkey fillets 4. Capon 5. Wing and leg joints 6. Roaster 7. Poussins 8. Breast of chicken 9. Drumstick 10. Wing tips 11. Duck 12. Goose*

plump and not too fatty, and the skin smooth. The flesh toughens once the bird is more than a year old. A goose weighs from 3½kg to 6½kg (7lb to 14lb) and will serve from five to ten portions.

**Duck and Duckling:** The beak on a fresh bird should be soft and pliable, the legs smooth and the webbing soft and easily torn. An average-sized duck weighing 1½kg to 2kg (3lb to 4lb) will serve four to six portions. You should allow one duckling for two portions.

When buying a frozen bird check that the skin is a good colour and the wrappings are not torn.

**Freezing:** Fresh well-packed chicken will keep for up to twelve months in the freezer—turkeys, ducks and geese will keep for up to six months.

## Cooking Poultry

All poultry can be roasted in the

Carving poultry

CHICKEN
*1. Hold leg with a napkin and cut through joint, pulling leg downwards and outwards to break it at the joint. If large, cut into two to separate the thigh and drumstick.*
*2. Cut through the wing joint, taking a slice from the breast.*
*3. Cut off the wishbone.*
*4. Slice breast parallel with the breastbone.*

TURKEY
*If large, carve as for goose; if small, carve as for chicken.*

DUCK
*1. Remove the leg as for chicken.*
*2. Remove wing.*
*3. Slice breast beginning just above the leg socket.*

GOOSE
*1. Slice from the leg as shown.*
*2. Slice breast, starting from the lowest part beside the leg.*

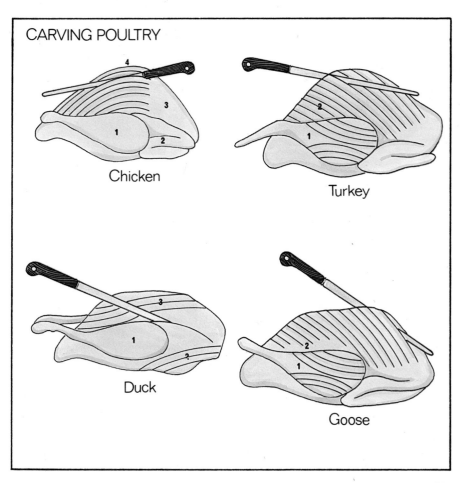

CARVING POULTRY

Chicken

Turkey

Duck

Goose

oven or on a spit, depending on size, and should be well-cooked. To ensure complete heat penetration of the body cavity, place most of the stuffing in the neck of the bird. If there is any extra stuffing, it may be placed in the body if necessary.

The breasts of chicken and turkey are dry meats, so cover them with fat before cooking to moisten the flesh. Duck and goose have very fatty flesh so cook these birds on a rack over a roasting tin to let the fat run out.

**Chicken:** Place in a roasting tin with fat bacon over the breast. Allow 25 minutes per ½kg (20 minutes per 1lb) and cook in a moderately hot oven (200 deg C, 400 deg F, Gas Mark 6), basting occasionally. Remove bacon to allow breast to brown for the last 15 minutes of cooking time.

Accompaniments: Forcemeat stuffing, bread sauce, bacon rolls, chipolata sausages.

**Turkey:** Cover breast with softened fat, wrap turkey in a double thickness of well greased greaseproof paper and tie with string. Place on shelf in centre of oven above roasting tin on the oven floor. Cook in a moderate oven (190 deg C, 375 deg F, Gas Mark 5) allowing 20 minutes per ½kg (15 minutes per 1lb), including stuffing for up to 6½kg (14lb) drawn weight, 15 minutes per ½kg (10 minutes per 1lb) for every ½kg (1lb) over 6½kg (14lb) drawn weight.

Accompaniments: Chestnut stuffing, forcemeat stuffing, chipolata sausages, bacon rolls, bread sauce.

**Duck:** Season inside of bird with salt and pepper and place on a wire rack in a roasting tin, without any fat; sprinkle with salt. Cook in a moderately hot oven (200 deg C, 400 deg F, Gas Mark 6) for 1 hour for a small duck or 20 minutes per ½kg (15 minutes per 1 lb) for a large duck.

Accompaniments: Sage and onion stuffing, apple sauce.

34

**Goose:** Place on a wire rack on a roasting tin, without any fat. Cook in a moderate oven (190 deg C, 375 deg F, Gas Mark 5) allowing 25 minutes per ½kg (20 minutes per 1lb). Pour fat from tin during cooking. If liked, for a crisp skin sprinkle breast with a little flour and raise oven temperature before the end of the cooking time.

Accompaniments: Sage and onion stuffing, apple and prune stuffing, apple sauce, redcurrant jelly, cranberry sauce.

Roasted boned chicken
Top left: *Cut the flesh away from the carcass, starting at the end tail.*
Top right: *Carefully scrape down the first leg bone to remove flesh.*
Middle left: *Scrape down the wing bone and turn the wing inside out.*
Middle right: *Gently ease the meat away from the breastbone.*
Bottom left: *Fold the boned chicken over to enclose the stuffing.*
Bottom right: *Close the skin of the chicken with thin string and trussing needle.*

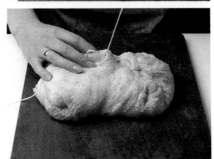

# ROASTED BONED CHICKEN
*For 6 to 8 portions*

1 chicken, about 1½kg (3lb) drawn weight

## Stuffing
6 rashers streaky bacon
6 slices white bread from a large loaf
1 medium-sized onion
1 × 2·5ml spoon (½ level teaspoon) mixed dried herbs
1 egg
Salt and pepper
Lard

1. Remove trussing string and giblets from chicken. Reserve chicken liver; place remainder of giblets in a medium-sized saucepan, cover with water and bring to boil. Cover and simmer. Rinse chicken and dry on kitchen paper.
2. To bone chicken: Place chicken,

breast downwards, with neck end facing away from you, on a board. Using a large, sharp knife, cut skin along backbone, from neck to tail. Cut off wing tips and tail; cut through bottom leg joint. Starting at tail end, gradually work flesh away from bones. When joint where leg joins body of chicken is exposed, cut through joint. Scrape down leg bones, turning legs inside out. When bones are removed from legs, continue working down body, making sure skin is not pierced. When wing joint is exposed cut through joint and work down wings, turning them inside out, as for legs. When the meat is attached to carcass only by the breast bone, gently ease meat away from bone with a knife.

**3.** Add chicken bones to giblets in saucepan; cover, return to boil and simmer for 1 hour. Reserve for gravy or soup.

**4.** Remove rind and bone from bacon; cut crusts from bread. Peel onion; cut into small pieces.

**5.** Mince bacon, reserved liver, onion and bread finely. Place in a bowl with herbs, egg, a little salt and a shake of pepper; mix well.

**6.** Prepare a moderately hot oven (200 deg C, 400 deg F, Gas Mark 6).

**7.** Lay chicken flat on a board, skin side downwards, leaving legs and wings turned inside out. Spread stuffing mixture down centre of chicken, over breast meat; fold chicken over, to enclose stuffing.

**8.** Using thin string and a trussing needle (or poultry pins), close skin of chicken; leave 15cm (6in) string each end.

**9.** Place chicken, join side downwards, in a roasting tin. Spread a little lard over chicken breast. Cook in centre of oven for 1 hour or until golden.

**10.** Remove from oven, pull out trussing string and place chicken on a warmed serving dish. Cut into thin slices and serve with new potatoes and a green vegetable. Alternatively, leave to cool, chill, then serve cold. Store in a fridge for up to 1 week or in a freezer for up to 3 months.

## WINTER CHICKEN WITH VEGETABLES
*For 4 portions*

1 chicken, (1½kg (3lb) drawn weight)
250g (½lb) button onions
250g (½lb) carrots
4 sticks of celery
1 chicken stock cube
25g (1oz) margarine
1×15ml (1 tablespoon) oil
2×15ml spoons (1 rounded tablespoon) plain flour
Pepper
Gravy browning
Salt

**1.** Prepare a moderate oven (190 deg C, 375 deg F, Gas Mark 5).

**2.** Remove giblets from chicken; place in saucepan, cover with water, bring to boil; simmer for 30 minutes.

**3.** Peel onions and carrots; cut carrots into quarters lengthwise. Wash celery and cut into 2cm (1in) lengths.

**4.** Strain giblet stock into a measuring jug and make up to 250ml (½ pint) with water, if necessary. Add chicken stock cube; stir until dissolved.

**5.** Heat margarine and oil in a large frying pan. Add chicken and fry until browned all over, turning frequently. Place chicken in a 2 litre (4 pint) casserole. Add vegetables to remaining fat in pan and fry for 5 minutes. Stir in flour, add stock and a shake of pepper. Bring to boil, stirring, and pour over chicken. Cover casserole and place in centre of oven. Cook for 1 hour until chicken and vegetables are tender.

**6.** Lift chicken on to a warmed serving dish, remove trussing string. Stir a little gravy browning into sauce, if desired. Taste and season with salt and pepper. Serve vegetables and gravy with chicken and boiled potatoes.

Below: *Winter chicken with vegetables*

## ROAST DUCK WITH ORANGE WINE SAUCE
*For 4 portions*

1 oven-ready duck
Salt
1 small and 2 medium-sized
  oranges

**Sauce**
1 small orange
1 small onion
1 rasher streaky bacon
Lard
1 × 15ml spoon (1 level tablespoon)
  plain flour
200ml (8 fluid oz) giblet stock
50ml (2 fluid oz) red wine
1 × 10ml spoon (1 rounded
  teaspoon) redcurrant jelly
Salt and pepper
Watercress or parsley

**1.** Prepare a moderately hot oven (200 deg C, 400 deg F, Gas Mark 6).
**2.** Remove giblets; rinse inside of duck with cold water and dry with kitchen paper. Place giblets in saucepan, cover with water, bring to boil and simmer for 1 hour. Drain and reserve 200ml (8 fluid oz) for sauce.
**3.** Weigh duck and calculate cooking time by allowing 20 minutes per ½kg (15 minutes per 1lb).
**4.** Truss duck with fine string then place it on a rack in a roasting tin, sprinkle with salt then cook in centre of oven for calculated time.
**5.** To make orange basket: using a sharp knife cut halfway down one side of centre from top of small orange. Cut in from side to meet downward cut and remove piece of orange. Repeat on other side of orange leaving a narrow strip in the centre to form handle. Using a teaspoon scoop out flesh from orange and reserve for sauce. Cut a zig-zag pattern around edge of basket with scissors.
**6.** Segment two medium-sized oranges: using a sharp or serrated knife cut peel and pith from fruit; cut out segments and reserve.
**7.** To make sauce: scrub orange, pare rind with a potato peeler or sharp knife. Shred half of pared rind and reserve; squeeze juice from orange and reserved flesh. Peel and chop onion. Remove rind and bone from bacon; chop bacon.
**8.** Melt a knob of lard in a medium-sized saucepan, add onion and bacon and fry for 3 to 4 minutes. Stir in flour and gradually add reserved stock, wine, orange juice and pared rind. Bring to boil, cover and simmer for 10 minutes. Place orange shreds in a small saucepan, cover them with water, bring to boil and cook for 5 minutes until tender; drain.
**9.** Strain sauce; add orange shreds and redcurrant jelly. Taste and season with salt and pepper.
**10.** Remove duck from oven and place on a warmed serving plate. Remove trussing string. Place orange segments around duck. Arrange sprigs of watercress or parsley in orange basket and place on serving plate. Reheat sauce and place in a warmed sauceboat.

Below: *Roast duck with orange wince sauce.*

## COUNTRY KITCHEN SOUP
*For 6 portions*

3 medium-sized leeks
100g (4oz) button mushrooms
2 large potatoes
50g (2oz) butter
50g (2oz) plain flour
¾ litre (1½ pints) turkey stock
250ml (½ pint) milk
1½ × 5ml spoons (1½ level
  teaspoons) salt
Pepper
1 × 15ml spoon (1 level tablespoon)
  chopped parsley

**1.** Trim roots, tops and any tough outside leaves from leeks. Cut leeks halfway through lengthwise, then open out and wash thoroughly to remove any soil; cut into rings. Wash and finely slice mushrooms.
**2.** Peel and thinly slice potatoes. Melt butter in a large saucepan, add potato slices and leeks and fry gently for 2 to 3 minutes, without browning. Add flour and continue cooking for 2 minutes.
**3.** Add turkey stock, milk, salt and a shake of pepper. Bring to boil, stirring; cover and simmer for 20 minutes. Add mushrooms and continue cooking for a further 5 minutes. Taste and add more salt and pepper if necessary.
**4.** To serve: pour soup into a a warmed tureen, sprinkled with chopped parsley.

*Note:* If turkey stock is not available, dissolve 2 chicken stock cubes in ¾ litre (1½ pints) boiling water, omit seasonings.

Right: *see key on page 38*

# Fish

There are so many varieties of fish available that there is something suitable for any meal. Fish is quick to cook, nutritious, and very versatile.

**Look for these points when buying:** Freshness is the key-note. Stale fish is unpleasant with a strong 'fishy' or ammonia smell and flavour. Whole fish should be firm with bright eyes. Choose fillets and steaks that are firm, elastic and white; avoid water or fibrous-looking fish. If the imprint of the fingers remains when the fish has been handled, then it is not fresh.

**Freezing:** Ideally, fish should be caught and frozen on the same day—definitely within twenty-four hours. The fish should be kept in ice or refrigerated after it is caught until it is frozen. Large fish should be gutted and cut into portions or filleted before freezing. Mackerel, herrings or whiting should be gutted—the heads can be left on if preferred. Pack individually in moisture-proof material, or glaze.

Fish, see page 37: *1. Skate 2. Smoked whiting 3. Whiting 4. Cod fillet 5. Cod steaks 6. Smoked cod 7. Herring 8. Buckling 9. Kippers 10. Saithe 11. Hake fillet and steaks 12. Plaice 13. Huss 14. Mackerel 15. Smoked haddock 16. Haddock fillet 17. Haddock steaks 18. Haddock smoked on bone*

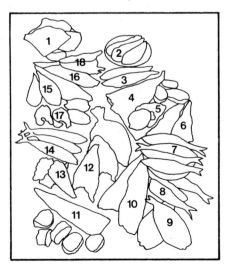

**To glaze:** Freeze fish, un-wrapped, until firm. Dip each fish in a bowl of icy salted water and place on a wire tray in freezer. Repeat several times until each fish is completely covered with ice. Over-wrap each fish in poly-thene and return to freezer.

# Cooking Fish

Avoid overcooking fish or it will be dry and tough. Most fish can be cooked by frying, grilling, poach-ing and baking. Some fat needs to be added to keep it moist.

**Frying:** Coat fish before frying and serve immediately after cooking.

1. Shallow frying: Coat fillets and steaks of white fish in seasoned flour, then fry in about 6mm ($\frac{1}{4}$in) oil and butter mixed for 5 to 10 minutes, depending on thickness. Allow 25g (1oz) butter to each 15ml (1 tablespoon) oil. Turn care-fully using a fish slice. To prevent fillets curling, cook fleshy side of fish first. Alternatively, coat fish in seasoned flour, then in beaten egg and browned or fresh bread-crumbs. Fry in oil or butter mixed with oil. Drain on crumpled kit-chen paper before serving.

2. Deep frying: Suitable for fillets that are not too thick. Coat portions of fish in seasoned flour, then in egg and breadcrumbs or batter. The fillets should be dipped in batter immediately before adding to the pre-heated fat. Fry small quantities at a time; drain on kitchen paper.

**Grilling:** This is the quickest and easiest way of cooking fish. To grill fillets and steaks, melt butter in grill pan, coat fish in seasoned flour and dip in butter. Turn over, arrange in pan and cook until golden brown, without turning. Lemon juice or mayon-naise stirred into the juices in the pan makes a quick sauce. To grill herrings and mackerel, score the skin of the whole, gutted fish, place in greased grill pan and cook

for about 10 minutes without added fat, turning carefully after 5 minutes.

**Poaching:** Ideal for smoked fish or where fish is served with a sauce. Use a large, shallow saucepan or a frying pan. Fill to 1cm ($\frac{1}{2}$in) depth with water, milk or a mixture of these. Place fish in pan, heat to just below boiling point and cook fish slowly. The liquid must never be allowed to boil or the fish will toughen. Carefully lift out fish and drain on kitchen paper. Use poach-ing liquor in a sauce to serve with the fish.

**Steaming:** An ideal method of cooking thin fillets of fine-grained fish, such as plaice and sole, especially suitable for invalids whose food needs to be easily digested. Place fillet on a buttered plate, cover with a lid or foil and place over a saucepan of boiling water; cook for about 10 minutes. A knob of butter may be placed on the fillet.

**Baking:** Suitable for whole fish, thick fillets and steaks. Various flavourings and toppings can be added, but white fish should be placed in an ovenproof dish and covered with a buttered paper to prevent drying. Steaks are de-licious topped with a flavoured butter and individually wrapped in foil.

## SAVOURY FISH TRIANGLES
*Makes 4*

$\frac{1}{4}$kg ($\frac{1}{2}$lb) huss, coley or cod
25g ($\frac{1}{2}$oz) margarine
25g ($\frac{1}{2}$oz) plain flour
125ml ($\frac{1}{4}$ pint) milk
1 small 198g (7oz) can sweet
   corn kernels
1 × 15ml spoon (1 level tablespoon)
   chopped parsley
1 × 5ml spoon (1 level teaspoon)
   salt
1 × 1·5ml spoon ($\frac{1}{4}$ level teaspoon
   pepper)
1 large 370g (13oz) packet frozen
   puff pastry, just thawed
Beaten egg to glaze

1. Prepare a moderately hot oven (200 deg C, 400 deg F, Gas Mark 6).
2. Remove bone and skin from fish if necessary; cut fish into 1.3cm ($\frac{1}{2}$in) pieces.
3. Melt margarine in a medium-sized saucepan; stir in flour and cook gently for about 2 minutes without browning. Add milk, bring to boil stirring continuously and cook for 2 minutes.
4. Remove from heat and stir in coley, drained sweetcorn, parsley, salt and pepper.
5. Roll out pastry on to a floured board and trim to a 30cm (12in) square. Cut square into 4 15cm (6in) squares.
6. Place a quarter of filling in centre of each square of pastry. Brush edges with water. Bring 2 opposite corners of one square together over filling to make a triangle; seal edges well. Place triangle, sealed edges sideways, on baking sheet. Repeat. Brush pastry with beaten egg; snip with scissors to decorate.
7. Cook just above centre of oven for 15 to 20 minutes, until well risen and golden brown. Serve with creamed potatoes and Brussels sprouts.

Top left: *Savoury fish triangles*

Left: *Tangy fish bake*

## TANGY FISH BAKE

*For 4 portions*

¾kg (1½lb) potatoes
Salt
½kg (1lb) coley, whiting or huss
4 gherkins
25g (1oz) margarine
25g (1oz) plain flour
250ml (½ pint) milk
4×15ml spoons (2 rounded
   tablespoons) salad cream
1×1·5ml spoon (¼ level teaspoon)
   pepper
2 large tomatoes
50g (2oz) Cheddar cheese
Sprig of parsley

1. Prepare a moderate oven (190 deg C, 375 deg F, Gas Mark 5).
2. Peel and slice potatoes; place in a saucepan of salted water. Bring to boil and cook for 2 minutes; drain.
3. Skin fish and remove bones, if necessary; cut fish into 2cm (1in) pieces. Cut gherkins into thin slices.
4. Melt margarine in a medium-sized saucepan; stir in flour and cook gently for about 2 minutes without browning. Add milk; bring to boil stirring continuously and cook for 2 minutes.
5. Stir in sliced gherkins, salad cream, fish, 5ml (1 level teaspoon) salt and pepper. Place in a 1 litre (2 pint) casserole. Slice the toma-toes; place on top of fish mixture. Arrange potatoes on top of toma-toes and sprinkle with salt.
6. Grate cheese and place over potatoes. Place casserole on a baking sheet; cook, uncovered, in centre of oven for 30 to 35 minutes until cheese is golden brown. Gar-nish with a sprig of parsley.

*Below: Kedgeree*

## KEDGEREE

*For 4 portions*

100g (4oz) long-grain rice
1 small (113g/¼lb) pack frozen
   peas
3 eggs
300g (¾lb) smoked haddock or
   cod
50g (2oz) butter
1×15ml spoon (1 tablespoon)
   top of the milk
Pepper
Sprigs of parsley

1. Cook rice in a large saucepan of boiling salted water for about 12 minutes. Add frozen peas 5 min-utes before end of cooking time. Test rice by pressing a grain between thumb and finger. Drain in a sieve or colander; rinse with boiling water.
2. Hard boil eggs for 10 minutes; crack and leave to cool in cold water. Shell and dry on kitchen paper. Cut 3 slices of egg for garnish and chop remainder.
3. Place fish in a frying pan. Cover with water, bring to boil, reduce heat and cook very slowly for 7 to 10 minutes. Drain, remove skin and any small bones; flake fish with a fork.
4. Melt butter in a large saucepan; stir in rice, fish, chopped eggs, top of the milk and ½×2·5ml spoon (¼ level teaspoon) pepper. When mixture is piping hot, place on a warmed serving plate. Place re-served sliced egg down centre of fish mixture and a sprig of parsley at each end. Serve immediately.

# Vegetable index

Vegetables are very versatile, served as an accompaniment to a main dish, a course by themselves or mixed with other ingredients. There are three main groups: green vegetables, the leaf and flower varieties, such as cabbage and cauliflower; roots and tubers, such as potatoes and carrots; and pulses, such as peas and beans. They are essential to a healthy, balanced diet since they provide a variety of nutrients. They all contain vitamins, mineral elements and roughage.

**Choice of Vegetables:** Stale vegetables, besides looking unhealthy, have less nutritional value. A stale vegetable will not improve with cooking, so always buy vegetables in peak condition. Greens should be bright and crisp and with not too many outside leaves; roots and tubers should be without excess soil or signs of softness and pulse vegetables should be as young as possible, when they will be tender.

**Keeping Vegetables:** Most vegetables freeze well; they must be blanched to retain their colour and nutrients. Some vegetables can be dried. Beans can be preserved by salting and vegetables may be bottled at home if a pressure cooker is used.

## Globe Artichokes

They are recognisable by their spiky leaves which surround an edible core known as the heart. Choose artichokes when young as the scales are fleshy and the heart tender. Prepare by cutting away the stem and larger outside leaves. Snip tip of each leaf to within 5cm (2in) of base. Cook in boiling, salted water for 15 to 20 minutes until the base is tender. To eat, pull off each leaf and dip fleshy end in melted butter or Hollandaise sauce. Scrape base of leaf between teeth to remove flesh. The heart will be left once the leaves are removed. This is also available separately in cans.

## Jerusalem Artichokes

These are root vegetables resembling mis-shapen potatoes; they have a delicate flavour. Always buy the largest available as there is a lot of wastage due to their knobbly shape. To prepare, scrub, peel and cook in boiling, salted water to which you have added a little juice, for 15 to 20 minutes. They may also be cooked in their skins, scrubbed, then boiled or steamed for about 15 to 20 minutes, until tender. The skins will then rub off easily. Serve with melted butter, white sauce or a cheese sauce. After parboiling they may be baked or roasted.

## Asparagus

This is usually sold in bundles of spears about 20cm to 23cm (8in to 9in) in length. Fat spears are the best quality but thin spindly spears known as sprue are sometimes available cheaply; they are useful for garnishing and flavouring cooked dishes. Scrape asparagus ends to remove tough skins and trim ends to an even length. Tie into bundles then place bundles upright in a saucepan. Cover lower two-thirds with salted water, bring to boil and simmer for 15 to 25 minutes, until tips are tender. Eat hot or cold with the fingers; dip tips in melted butter or Hollandaise sauce then discard woody part of each stem.

## Aubergine or Egg Plant

It has an attractive glossy deep purple skin. Wrinkled skins indicate old age and should be avoided. There are also yellow, white, green and brown varieties, but these are not often available. They may be peeled but are attractive with the dark skin left on. Cut into cubes or slices and sprinkle with salt to remove some of the water that they naturally contain; leave for 20 minutes, drain, then fry or bake. Alternatively serve halved aubergines stuffed with a savoury meat mixture, or bake whole.

## Broad Beans

These are the first of the summer vegetables. When very young, both the pods and the beans can be sliced and cooked. More mature beans need to be podded and 350g to 450g ($\frac{3}{4}$lb to 1lb) of beans must be bought for each portion. Cook in very little boiling, salted water for a few minutes until tender. Serve with a knob of butter.

## French Beans

To indicate freshness these should snap easily when broken. They should be cooked whole, or cut into chunks, in a little boiling, salted water for 10 to 15 minutes or until tender.

## Runner Beans

These should be bought when young and tender as they become tough and stringy when old. Remove strings around side with a sharp knife then slice. Cook in a little boiling, salted water until just tender.

## Broccoli

This resembles a cross between a cabbage and a cauliflower. Choose fresh broccoli with firm buds that are compact and strongly coloured deep green or purple. Cook in a little boiling, salted water until just tender. Serve with melted

Top: *Cabbage, cauliflower, broccoli, spinach*

Centre: *Onions, swede, artichokes, carrots*

Bottom: *Peppers, potatoes, aubergines, asparagus*

butter as a vegetable accompaniment, or Hollandaise sauce for a starter.

## Brussels Sprouts

Bright, closely packed leaves indicate freshness. Remove outer leaves and cook in a little boiling, salted water for 10 to 15 minutes.

## Cabbage

There are many varieties of cabbage available throughout the year. The Spring cabbage is recognisable by clusters of crisp,

crinkly leaves around a conical shaped heart. Primo cabbage is a popular summer variety and Savoy a winter variety. Red cabbage and white Dutch cabbages have tightly packed leaves. Prepare cabbage by removing the outer leaves and stem and washing carefully. Cook finely shredded leaves in a little boiling, salted water for 5 to 10 minutes.

## Carrots

They should look fresh, bright and well-shaped with smooth skins. Old carrots tend to be woody when cooked. Peel and slice mature carrots and cook in boiling, salted water for 15 to 20 minutes. Alternatively cook carrots in a covered casserole with a knob of butter and a little water. Scrub tender new carrots and cook whole by steaming

or boil in the minimum of water for 15 to 20 minutes. They are delicious grated, raw in salads.

## Cauliflower

This is developed for the sake of its flower—sometimes called curd. The stalk base should be white and clean with crisp, fresh leaves covering a firm, odourless curd. A cauliflower should be bought with the leaves covering the curd if it needs to be stored. To keep it white, cook whole or cut into sprigs in boiling, salted water for about 10 minutes, or until tender. Serve coated with a thick white sauce. Break off small florets and serve raw in salads.

## Celery

It should be bought when the

sticks are smooth with a plump, healthy looking base. Sliced celery makes a crisp addition to a salad and it is delicious served in sticks with cheese. It may also be braised and served as a hot vegetable or with a cheese sauce for a supper dish. You will find that it is a useful vegetable for flavouring soups and stews.

## Chicory

Chicory should have plump, tightly packed clusters of white leaves with yellowing tips. Avoid chicory with green tips, which indicate that it has been kept in the light and that it will be stale and bitter. Trim outside leaves, then cook whole in boiling, salted water for about 10 minutes. Drain and serve with a knob of butter or coat in a white sauce. Chicory has very

crisp leaves and is quite delicious when sliced and served raw in salads.

## Corn-on-the-cob

This is a sweet vegetable that is very versatile once cooked. It is available fresh in early summer but is also available frozen and in cans. The outer sheathing leaves of a fresh corn should be green with silky tassels; the corn kernels should be soft and milky when pressed. To cook, trim off leaves and silk and cook whole cobs in plenty of boiling, salted water for 5 to 8 minutes, until tender; overcooking tends to toughen the cob. Serve with lots of melted butter, as a vegetable or as a starter. The cooked corn, stripped from the cob, is delicious in salads, flans and fritters.

Top: *Jerusalem artichokes, French beans peas, turnip, parsnip*
Centre: *Chicory, Brussels sprouts, corn-on-the-cob, leeks, white cabbage*
Bottom: *Mushrooms, celery, red cabbage, courgettes*

## Courgettes or Zucchini

These should be 10cm to 15cm (4in to 6in) long, evenly coloured green and firm. Small courgettes may be cooked whole and larger ones sliced or slit lengthwise and fried in butter until tender.

## Leeks

This is the oldest recorded British vegetable. A fresh leek is slim with a white stalk and clean, green leaves. Old leeks develop hard cores which grow from the centre and have an acrid taste when cooked. Trim roots, tops and any

43

tough outside leaves from leeks. Cut leeks halfway through lengthwise. Open out and wash thoroughly to remove any soil. Cook whole or cut into rings in boiling, salted water for 10 to 15 minutes or until tender. Serve with a knob of butter as an accompanying vegetable or coated in cheese sauce for a main meal with rashers of bacon.

## Marrow or Squash

The skin should have a dull shine and it should be just soft enough to yield to the pressure of a finger. Peel, slice or cut in half lengthwise and remove centre pith and seeds. Marrow should be cooked in the minimum of liquid as it contains a high proportion of water. It is best cooked until just tender in melted butter in a covered saucepan or casserole. Overcooking makes it flabby and tasteless. Halved marrows may be stuffed with a savoury meat mixture and baked.

## Mushrooms

Almost all mushrooms are cultivated nowadays and are available in various sizes. The smallest mushroom, the button, should be lightly fried in butter or grilled to serve as a vegetable. It can be added to egg-based flans, used in sauces or cooked with meat or fish. The cup mushroom is ideal for stuffing and flat mushrooms may be added to soups, casseroles, or lightly fried in butter to serve as a vegetable. Store in a covered container or polythene bag in the fridge.

## Onions

Choose onions that are firm and full. Old onions with shoots growing from the top should be avoided. Spanish onions are the largest variety; they have a mild flavour which makes them ideal for eating raw and serving sliced in salads. The smaller the onion the stronger the flavour; for example, choose shallots and pickling onions for preserving in vinegar. Mildly flavoured spring onions resemble thin leeks and need only topping and tailing before adding salads. Onions may be cooked in a great many ways: fried in rings with or without butter; boiled whole; parboiled and roasted around the joint; baked whole, stuffed with a savoury meat or cheese mixture; as a flavouring for soups, sauces and stews or as an integral part of many savoury meals.

## Parsnips

Aged parsnips become wizened and woody. Buy them with fresh roots and no distinctive brown patches. Peel and cut in rings, dice or cut in fingers and cook in boiling, salted water for 15 to 20 minutes, or until tender. Drain, mash with butter and pepper, if desired, or parboil and roast around the joint.

## Peas

It is well worth the trouble of shelling fresh peas because of their delicious and unique flavour. Cook for 5 to 8 minutes in a little boiling, salted water, drain, add a knob of butter and serve immediately. Peas have a very short season and so are available in many processed forms. Frozen peas are picked when young and tender and frozen immediately. Quick-dried peas are young, sweet peas that are dried by a special process. Marrowfat peas are large peas that are left to mature on the vine then picked when dry. They are available dry, canned and frozen.

## Sweet Peppers

These are also known as capsicums or pimentos. They come in various colours: red, green and sometimes yellow. They are attractive and should be crisp, firm and glossy skinned. They are best bought as required as they soon lose their crispness and vitamin C, of which they are a valuable source. Peppers are delicious with pith and seeds removed, cut into slices, rings or cubes and added to salads, or blanched and added to sauces and main dishes. They can also be cooked whole and stuffed. Peppers are available frozen, canned and bottled as well as fresh.

## Potatoes

Many varieties of potato are available throughout the year. Choose the variety best suited to the way it is to be cooked—for example, the King Edward is an all purpose potato which has a slightly floury texture; the Majestic is best for frying and the Redskin for soups and jacket baking. Buy potatoes clean, soil free and free from brown or unnatural marks.

## Spinach

This should be delicately leafed with no bruising. It is a valuable source of iron and vitamins B and C. Wash spinach thoroughly to remove grit and cut away any tough stems. Place in a large saucepan with only the water adhering to the leaves and cook, covered, over a low heat until tender, about 10 minutes. Pour spinach into a sieve and press out water, return to saucepan and reheat with melted butter, salt, black pepper and nutmeg. Chop with a knife or press through a sieve to make a purée, if desired.

## Swede

This is an economical root vegetable. Make sure the skin is soil-free and unwrinkled. Peel thickly and cook as for parsnips. Useful in soups, stews and casseroles.

## Turnip

This is an oval shaped root vegetable. Peel, cut into chunks and cook in a little boiling, salted water for 15 to 20 minutes, or until tender, then serve with a knob of butter. Mix with other root vegetables for a delicious purée. Turnip tops, the sprouting leaves, are a delicious vegetable on their own.

44

# Eggs

Eggs are the original 'convenience food': they come hygienically packed in their own conveniently-sized containers and can be ready to eat in three minutes. Eggs contain all the nutrients essential for life—protein, fats, vitamins and even a small amount of carbohydrate. Eggs should be kept well away from the ice box, if storing them in a refrigerator; either keep them in their boxes at the bottom of the refrigerator or in the egg racks provided in some models. The rounded end of the egg should be uppermost during storage. Egg shells are porous, so keep eggs away from strong-smelling foods like fish, cheese and onions. Allow eggs to come to room temperature before using. When a really fresh egg is broken on to a plate, the yolk is supported by a thick, compact white. As the egg becomes stale, the white becomes thinner and spreads.

Eggs are one of the most versatile ingredients used in everyday cookery and are a main ingredient of innumerable dishes. They are also delicious just boiled in their shells; this, incidentally, is an art in itself—in fact, they should not be 'boiled' at all, but simmered. Fast boiling spoils the flavour and makes the whites tough. The length of time to cook soft-boiled eggs is a matter of personal preference. To hard boil eggs successfully, cook large eggs for 12 minutes and standard eggs for 10 minutes; crack and leave to cool in cold, running water, then shell and dry on kitchen paper. Hard-boiled eggs that have dark rings around the yolk have either been cooked too long or have not been cracked and cooled quickly, so have gone on cooking in their shells. The dark ring is iron sulphide, which is quite harmless.

*Right: Stuffed eggs with cabbage*

## STUFFED EGGS WITH CABBAGE
*For 4 portions*

8 eggs
½kg (1lb) cabbage
1 chicken extract cube
1 small onion
25g (1oz) margarine
25g (1oz) plain flour
250ml (½ pint) milk
A little dry mustard
5ml (1 level teaspoon) salt
Pepper
50g (2oz) Cheddar cheese

1. Hard boil eggs for 10 minutes; crack and leave to cool in cold water. Shell and dry on kitchen paper. Cut in halves lengthwise; remove egg yolks and place in a basin.
2. Remove outside leaves from cabbage and discard; wash and shred cabbage. Place chicken extract cube and 125ml (¼ pint) water in a saucepan; bring to boil, stirring, until extract cube has dissolved. Add cabbage and cook for 6 to 8 minutes, until tender; drain.
3. Peel and chop onion. Melt margarine in a medium-sized saucepan; add onion and cook for 3 to 4 minutes, until soft, but not browned. Stir in flour and cook for 1 minute, without browning. Add milk; bring to boil, stirring continuously. Add mustard, salt and a shake of pepper; cook for 1 minute. Remove from heat and beat a little sauce into egg yolks.
4. Grate cheese; stir half of cheese into sauce and cover sauce with a piece of wet greaseproof paper, to prevent a skin forming.
5. Sandwich pairs of egg halves together with egg-yolk mixture. Place eggs in centre of a shallow ovenproof dish. Prepare a low grill. Place dish under grill, to warm eggs.
6. Reheat sauce; pour over eggs in dish. Sprinkle with remaining cheese. Place under a moderate grill, until cheese is golden brown. Remove from grill and place a little cabbage at ends of dish. Serve remainder separately.

## SPINACH SOUFFLÉ
*For 4 portions*

1 (200/8oz) packet frozen chopped
   spinach, just thawed
Milk
50g (2oz) soft margarine
50g (2oz) plain flour
A little nutmeg
15ml (1 level tablespoon)
   Parmesan cheese
2·5ml (½ level teaspoon) salt
Pepper
4 eggs

1. Prepare a moderate oven (190 deg C, 375 deg F, Gas Mark 5). Brush the inside of a 16cm (6½in) soufflé dish with melted margarine.
2. Place spinach in a sieve over a basin and press lightly, to extract excess water. Place the spinach in a measuring jug; make up to ½ pint with milk.
3. Place spinach mixture, margarine, flour, nutmeg, Parmesan cheese, salt and a shake of pepper in a medium-sized saucepan. Bring to boil, stirring, and cook for 2 minutes. Leave sauce to cool slightly.
4. Separate eggs; place whites in a clean, grease-free bowl and beat yolks into sauce.
5. Whisk egg whites, until stiff, but not dry. Using a metal spoon, carefully fold egg whites into sauce. Pour into prepared dish. Place soufflé on a baking sheet and cook in centre of oven for 25 to 30 minutes, until well risen and golden brown. Serve immediately with cabbage salad and tomatoes.

## VEGETABLE OMELET
*For 4 portions*

**Filling**
1 medium-sized onion
1 medium-sized carrot
1 medium-sized potato
4 medium-sized mushrooms
1 × 15ml spoon (1 tablespoon) oil
4 × 15ml spoons (2 rounded
   tablespoons) cooked peas
3 eggs
Salt and pepper
25g (1oz) grated Cheddar cheese

1. Peel and chop onion. Peel carrot and potato; cut into small dice. Wash and slice mushrooms.
2. Heat oil in a small saucepan. Add onion, potato and carrot; cook slowly for 8 to 10 minutes, until vegetables are tender. Stir in mushrooms, peas.
3. Place eggs and a little salt and pepper in a basin. Beat with a fork until just mixed.
4. Heat a little oil slowly in an 21.5cm (8½in) omelet or frying pan, swirl to coat pan, then pour in egg mixture from basin. Cook slowly, until underside is nearly set. Add filling and cook until egg mixture is set. Sprinkle with cheese. Serve with creamed potatoes.

## ZABAGLIONE
*For 4 portions*

4 egg yolks
4 × 10ml spoons (4 rounded
   teaspoons) castor sugar
4 × 15ml spoons (4 tablespoons)
   marsala or sherry

1. Place a deep bowl over a saucepan of hot, but not boiling, water.
2. Add egg yolks, sugar and marsala or sherry and beat with a rotary whisk until the mixture has trebled in bulk. Pour into small glasses and serve immediately, with crisp, sweet biscuits.

Right: *see key on page 48*

Below: *Vegetable omelet*

# Dairy matters

Milk is a very versatile food, which can be used as a basis for an almost endless variety of dishes. Ordinary pasteurised milk is usually chosen for cooking, beverages, and cereals. Sterilised milk makes a creamy, slightly caramel-flavoured rice pudding, but sterilised or UHT milk will not set junket.

**Milk puddings:** Use 50g (1½oz) short grain rice, sago, or tapioca and 2 × 15ml spoons (2 level tablespoons) sugar to 570ml (1 pint) milk.

**Junket:** Use 1 × 5ml spoon (1 teaspoon) flavoured or plain rennet to 570ml (1 pint) milk.

**Pouring batter:** Use 100g (4oz) plain flour, ½ × 2·5ml spoon (¼ level teaspoon) salt, 1 egg and 250ml (½ pint) milk.

**Coating batter:** As above, but use only 125ml (¼ pint) milk.

**Pouring sauces:** 25g (1oz) margarine and 25g (1oz) plain flour to 250ml (½ pint) milk.

**Coating sauces:** 50g (2oz) margarine and 50g (2oz) plain flour to 570ml (1 pint) milk.

**Binding sauces:** 100g (4oz) margarine and 100 g (4oz) plain flour to 570ml (1 pint) milk.

Dairy, see page 47: *1. Natural and flavoured yoghourt 2. Curd cheese 3. Natural cottage cheese 4. Crowdie 5. Cottage cheese with chives 6. Full-fat cream cheese 7. Clotted cream 8. UHT milk in a Tetrapack 9. Whipped double cream 10. Single cream 11. Buttermilk 12. 'Long-keeping' cream 13. Sterilised milk 14, 15, 16. Pasteurised milk*

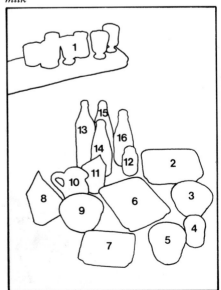

## Cooking with Cream

Fresh cream enriches the flavour and quality of many sweet and savoury dishes. Half, single and sterilised half creams are pouring creams used in coffee, sauces and soups, and also on cereals and fruit. For perfect whipped cream used in dishes such as trifles, gateaux and fruit flans, make sure the cream, whisk and bowl are really cold. Add 1 × 15ml spoon (1 tablespoon) milk to each 125ml (¼ pint) double cream or use half double and half single cream. Whisk the cream quickly at first, until it appears matt, then slowly until it stands in peaks. Take care not to over-whip as it will turn to butter.

## Cultured Milk

Cultured buttermilk has a buttermilk culture added to skimmed milk to produce a delightful and refreshing drink with a slightly acid flavour. It is also used for making scones.

Soured cream has a piquant and refreshing taste, which can enhance the flavour and creaminess of many made dishes. Stir a tablespoonful into soup before serving. If soured cream is not available, add 1 × 5ml spoon (1 teaspoon) fresh lemon juice to 125ml (¼ pint) of single cream to give a similar sharpness and flavour.

## Yoghourt

Yoghourt is thought to have originated among the nomadic tribes of Eastern Europe. Traditionally it was a drink, made by allowing the natural milk flora to ferment the milk sugar to lactic acid, giving a very sour yoghourt.

Yoghourt contains all the nutrients which are found in milk, and is easily digested. It is particularly suitable for children, the elderly and people who have digestive ailments.

Yoghourt, unless pasteurised after preparation, contains 'live' bacteria which, when kept at a low temperature, remain dormant.

They increase the acidity when the temperature is raised, so keep yoghourt in a refrigerator.

## Cooking with Yoghourt

To give casseroles, stews, soups or gravies a tangy flavour, add some natural yoghourt just before serving. Do not allow to boil, as the yoghourt could curdle. For a refreshing start to the day, try natural or fruit yoghourt on cereals or muesli. It is delicious served with fruit for dessert, and is useful for slimmers' meals. Replace milk with yoghourt in plain cake or scone mixtures. You can also use natural yoghourt for a quick salad dressing—it is particularly delicious with cucumber.

## Cheese

Cheese can be found indigestible by some people because it is such a concentrated form of food, but as long as it is eaten in conjunction with other foods or cooked to adjust its concentrated food form, these digestive problems need never arise. The protein in cheese is covered by fat which prevents the digestive juices in the stomach from dealing immediately with the protein. However, grating and mixing cheese with sauce to absorb the fat, and the addition of seasonings, such as mustard, help the digestive juices to deal with the protein more easily. If cheese is overcooked it will become leathery and tough, so cook over a gentle heat for as short a time as possible.

**Look for these points when buying Cheese:** All varieties of cheese should have even texture as cracks will show that the cheese has been allowed to become dry, causing loss of flavour. Surface moisture or sweating should always be avoided as a moist surface is an ideal breeding ground for bacteria and mould. When buying a coloured cheese, check that the colour is not mottled. Vacuum-packed or film wrapped cheese should always have a clear wrapping. Cloudiness shows that air has entered the packet which could contaminate the cheese inside. Always check the 'sell by' date of pre-packed cheeses.

## Cooking with Soft Cheese

Cream, curd and cottage cheeses are the types most often used in cooking. In varying proportions, they can make a variety of different flavoured and textured cheese-cakes. For salads, try natural cottage cheese on its own, or with chopped parsley, celery, cooked meat, hard-boiled eggs, or canned tuna. Jacket potatoes are delicious split open and topped with cottage cheese. Cream and curd cheese make excellent party dips and sandwich spreads. When beaten with a little cream and flavouring, cream cheese can be used for piping decorations on sweet and savoury dishes. Add cottage or curd cheese to the fillings of savoury flans.

## Freezing

Ordinary pasteurised milk does not freeze well, though homogenised milk can be frozen for up to one month. Cottage cheese is not suitable for freezing. To freeze successfully, cream needs to contain at least 35 per cent butterfat. Whipping and double cream can be frozen for up to three months. Best results are obtained if the cream is lightly whipped first. If the cream is to be used for sweet dishes, add 1 × 5ml spoon (1 teaspoon) castor sugar to 125ml ($\frac{1}{4}$ pint) cream, to avoid separation.

For decorating cakes and desserts, pipe stars of cream on to a tray, open freeze, then pack in containers. Place on cake or dessert while still frozen.

Fruit yoghourts will freeze satisfactorily for up to six weeks, but natural and home-made yoghourt do not freeze successfully.

Most hard cheeses freeze very well. Four to six months is their usual freezer life.

## CHILLED CUCUMBER SOUP
*For 4 portions*

---

1 medium-sized cucumber
1 chicken stock cube
Salt and pepper
125ml ($\frac{1}{4}$ pint) chilled milk
1 (150g/5 fluid oz) carton
   natural yoghourt

---

**1.** Wash and trim cucumber, if necessary. Cut 3 thin slices of cucumber and reserve. Roughly chop remainder.
**2.** Place cucumber, chicken stock cube and 375ml ($\frac{3}{4}$ pint) water in a medium saucepan. Bring to boil, cover and simmer for 10 minutes, until cucumber is soft.
**3.** Remove from heat. Using a wooden spoon, press cucumber through a sieve into a soup tureen, or liquidise in an electric blender, then strain. Add 1 × 2·5ml spoon ($\frac{1}{2}$ level teaspoon) salt and a shake of pepper, leave until cold, then chill in the refrigerator.
**4.** Stir in milk and yoghourt. Taste and season, if necessary. Place the reserved slices of cucumber on top of soup and serve with croûtons.

Top: *Chilled cucumber soup*

Bottom: *Vanilla ice-cream*

## VANILLA ICE CREAM
*For 6 portions*

---

1 × 15ml spoon (1 level tablespoon) custard powder
3 × 15ml spoons (3 level tablespoons) castor sugar
250ml (½ pint) milk
1 × 5ml spoon (1 teaspoon) vanilla essence
1 (142ml/5 fluid oz) carton double cream

---

1. Turn refrigerator to the coldest setting.
2. Blend together custard powder, sugar and a little of the measured milk in a basin. Place remaining milk in a medium-sized saucepan and bring to boil. Pour on to blended custard powder and return to pan; bring to boil, stirring, and cook for 1 minute. Remove from heat and stir in vanilla essence. Cover with a piece of dampened greaseproof paper, wet side downwards, and place pan in a bowl of cold water to cool.
3. Place cream in a basin, and whisk until it just holds its shape. Fold custard into cream and pour into a freezing tray or plastic tray. Cover with foil or self-clinging plastic wrap and leave in the frozen food compartment until partially set—about 1 to 1½ hours.
4. Remove ice cream from refrigerator, scrape into a chilled bowl and whisk until mixture is smooth. Return to tray and re-freeze for 1 hour, or until firm. Turn refrigerator back to normal setting.

*Note:* For coffee ice cream, omit vanilla essence and add 1 × 15ml spoon (1 level tablespoon) instant coffee to custard powder and sugar.

For chocolate ice cream, omit vanilla essence and add 1 × 5ml spoon (1 level teaspoon) cocoa to custard powder and sugar and 25g (1oz) plain chocolate to the cooked custard. Stir until chocolate has dissolved.

## CRÈME CARAMEL
*For 4 portions*

---

50g (2oz) granulated sugar
Custard
4 eggs
375ml (¾ pint) milk
50g (2oz) granulated sugar
1 × 2·5ml spoon (½ teaspoon) vanilla essence

---

1. Prepare a very cool oven (140 deg C, 275 deg F, Gas Mark 1). Half-fill a roasting tin with warm water.
2. Warm a 725ml (1¼ pint) soufflé dish. Place 50g (2oz) granulated sugar and 2 × 15ml spoons (2 tablespoons) water in a thick saucepan and heat slowly until sugar has dissolved. Bring to boil and boil steadily, without stirring, until sugar turns a deep golden brown. Pour into warmed dish and leave for 2 minutes to set, then place dish in the water bath.
3. Beat eggs in a basin. Place milk and 50g (2oz) sugar in a saucepan and heat until almost boiling. Add to eggs, with vanilla essence and beat lightly.
4. Strain egg and milk mixture on to the caramel. Place roasting tin containing dish in the centre of oven, and cook for 1 hour or until custard is set and lightly browned on top. Remove dish from roasting tin and leave until custard is quite cold, about 3 hours or overnight. Loosen edge of custard by gently pulling towards centre with the fingers; invert on to a serving plate.

*Note:* For individual crème caramels, divide caramel and custard between 4 pottery teacups and cook for about 40 minutes.

For a vanilla baked custard, omit caramel and add a few drops vanilla essence. Pour custard into dish and sprinkle with a little grated nutmeg; serve in dish.

Right: *Crème caramel*

## POURING BATTER
**Used for pancakes, Yorkshire pudding and Toad-in-the-Hole.**

100g (4oz) plain flour
½ × 2·5ml spoon (¼ level teaspoon) salt
1 egg
250ml (½ pint) milk and water, mixed

**1.** Place flour and salt in a bowl. Make a 'well' in centre of flour and add egg. Stir in half the milk and water mixture. Mix well, using a wooden spoon, and beat until smooth. Add remainder of milk and water, then use as required.

### Pancakes
**1.** Place batter in a jug. Heat a little lard in a medium-sized frying pan. Pour any excess lard into a small basin, leaving pan lightly greased. Pour sufficient batter into pan, swirling quickly, to coat pan thinly. Cook until underside is golden brown.
**2.** Hold pan over a sheet of sugared paper (in case of accidents) and slip pancake to side of pan opposite handle. Quickly toss, or flip over with a palette knife. Cook over a moderate heat until brown.
**3.** Invert pancake on to a sheet of sugared paper, sprinkle with lemon juice and roll up, using 2 forks. Place on a hot ovenproof serving dish. Put in a warm oven; use remaining batter to make more pancakes.

### Yorkshire Pudding
**1.** Prepare a hot oven (230 deg C, 450 deg F, Gas Mark 8). Place a little lard in 12 individual Yorkshire pudding tins (or bun tins), or a 18cm (7in) square tin; place in oven until fat is hot.
**2.** Pour batter in tins (or tin) and bake on shelf in top of oven for 10 to 15 minutes, if using individual tins, or 30 to 40 minutes, if using a large tin, until risen and golden brown.

### Toad-in-the-Hole
Prepare a hot oven (220 deg C, 425 deg F, Gas Mark 7). Place lard and 450g (1lb) sausages in a 28cm by 18cm (11in by 7in) roasting tin. Place on shelf in top of oven, until lard is hot. Pour batter over sausages, replace in oven and cook for 35 to 40 minutes, until well risen and golden brown.

## SAVOURY BREAD AND BUTTER PUDDING
*For 4 portions*

6 slices bread from a large white loaf
50g (2oz) softened butter
150g (6oz) cheese
1 small (150g/5½oz) can pilchards in tomato sauce
2 eggs
250ml (½ pint) milk
1 × 2·5ml spoon (½ level teaspoon) salt
Pepper
1 × 2·5ml spoon (½ level teaspoon) dry mustard
Parsley

**1.** Cut crusts from bread, butter each slice and cut each into 4 triangles. Grate cheese and open can of pilchards.
**2.** Butter a 1-litre (2-pint) ovenproof pie dish. Arrange a layer of bread and spread contents of can of pilchards over bread with a fork. Layer remaining cheese and top with the remaining bread, buttered side up.
**3.** Beat eggs in a bowl. Place milk, salt, a shake of pepper and mustard in a small saucepan and heat through. Pour on to eggs and mix well. Strain over pudding and leave for 30 minutes for bread to soak.
**4.** Prepare a moderate oven (180 deg C, 350 deg F, Gas Mark 4).
**5.** Place pudding in centre of oven and bake for 1 to 1¼ hours. Remove from oven and sprinkle with chopped parsley. Serve for a main meal with a green vegetable and jacket potatoes cooked alongside pudding.

*Below: Savoury bread and butter pudding*

## WELSH RAREBIT
*For 4 portions*

2 tablespoons milk
25g (1oz) margarine
1×10ml spoon (2 teaspoons)
 Worcestershire sauce
1×5ml spoon (1 level teaspoon)
 dry mustard
$\frac{1}{2}$×2·5ml spoon ($\frac{1}{4}$ level teaspoon)
 salt
$\frac{1}{2}$×2·5ml ($\frac{1}{4}$ teaspoon) pepper
150g (6oz) Cheddar cheese
1 (20cm/8in) piece from a French
 loaf
Watercress
Tomato quarters

1. Prepare a hot grill.
2. Place milk, margarine, Worcestershire sauce, mustard, salt and pepper in a small saucepan and heat; do not boil. Cool slightly.
3. Grate cheese and add to saucepan; beat until smooth.
4. Cut bread in half and then slice through. Spread cut side thickly with cheese mixture. Grill for 2 to 3 minutes until golden brown.
5. Serve piping hot with watercress and tomato quarters.

*Note :* Cider or beer may be substituted for milk. Cheese mixture may be made in advance and stored in a plastic container in a refrigerator for up to 1 week.

Below: *Welsh rarebit*

## DANISH BLUE CHEESE PÂTÉ
*For 6 to 8 portions*

300g (12oz) Danish Blue cheese
125g (5oz) demi-sel cheese
1×5ml spoon (1 level teaspoon)
 grated onion
75g (3oz) margarine or butter
Pinch of Cayenne pepper
1×10ml (2 teaspoons)
 Worcestershire sauce
50g (2oz) salted peanuts
Sprigs of watercress
A little lettuce

1. Line a 450g (1lb) loaf tin with greaseproof paper.
2. Sieve Danish Blue cheese into a bowl. Add demi-sel cheese, grated onion, margarine or butter, Cayenne pepper and Worcester-

Above : *Danish blue cheese pâté*

shire sauce; mix thoroughly.
3. Press cheese mixture into lined tin, level top and cover with greaseproof paper. Place in refrigerator; leave for several hours or overnight.
4. Coarsely chop peanuts; place them on a plate.
5. Turn out cheese pâté and remove paper. Using a palette knife, press nuts on to sides, ends and top of pâté. Place pâté on a board; garnish with sprigs of watercress and lettuce leaves. Serve with hot buttered toast or melba toast and butter.

*Note :* Alternatively, pâté may be cut into thick slices and arranged on individual plates. Garnish with lettuce leaves and wedges of tomato.

## PARMESAN SHORTCAKES
*Makes 18*

150g (6oz) plain flour
50g (2oz) lard
50g (2oz) margarine
Grated Parmesan cheese
Pinch of Cayenne pepper
$\frac{1}{2}$×2·5ml spoon ($\frac{1}{4}$ level teaspoon)
 celery salt

1. Prepare a moderate oven (180 deg C, 350 deg F, Gas Mark 4). Lightly grease a shallow, 18cm (7in) square tin.
2. Place flour in a bowl. Add fats, cut into small pieces, and rub in with the fingertips until mixture resembles fine breadcrumbs. Mix in 25g (1oz) grated cheese, Cayenne pepper and celery salt.
3. Turn out mixture into tin; level top and press down lightly.
4. Bake in centre of oven for 35 to 40 minutes, or until pale golden brown.
5. Remove from oven; sprinkle with a little more grated Parmesan cheese and leave to cool for 10 minutes. Cut into 6 bars; cut each bar into 3 equal pieces. Leave to cool completely in the tin.
6. Remove from tin and serve with tomato or vegetable soup.

# Desserts

## FRUIT APPLE PIE
*For 4 to 6 portions*

---

½kg (1lb) cooking apples
Granulated sugar

**Shortcrust Pastry**
200g (8oz) plain flour
1 × 2·5ml spoon (½ level teaspoon) salt
50g (2oz) lard
50g (2oz) margarine
Cold water to mix

---

**1.** Prepare a moderately hot oven (200 deg C, 400 deg F, Gas Mark 6).
**2.** Peel, core and slice apples; sprinkle with 6 × 15ml spoons (3 rounded tablespoons) sugar.
**3.** Place flour and salt in a bowl. Add fats, cut into small pieces; rub in with the fingertips until mixture resembles fine breadcrumbs. Add about 2 × 15ml spoons (2 tablespoons) water and mix with a fork to form a firm dough.
**4.** Turn out on to a floured board and knead lightly. Divide pastry into 2 and roll out one half to line a 20.5cm (8in) ovenproof plate.

Brush edge of pastry with water.
**5.** Arrange apples on pastry. Roll out remaining pastry, and lift it, over the rolling pin, on to apples. Seal the edges well, trim, then cut with back of a knife to thicken; pinch edges to decorate. Make a small hole in centre of pie to enable steam to escape.
**6.** Brush top with a little cold water, sprinkle with granulated sugar. Place pie on a baking sheet and bake in centre of oven for 35 to 40 minutes until apple is soft and pastry lightly browned.

*Perfect Pastry Tips*
**1.** Rub in thoroughly; the fat must be cool and firm.
**2.** Add about 1 × 5ml spoon (1 teaspoon) of water to each 25g (1oz) flour, just sufficient to make a firm dough. Too much water would make the pastry hard; with too little water, the pastry would be crumbly and difficult to handle.
**3.** Avoid stretching the pastry when rolling out, as it may shrink in cooking.

Below: *Apple pie*

## CHOCOLATE RUM PIE

---

**Coconut Pastry**
150g (6oz) plain flour
75g (3oz) mixed cooking fats
1 × 2·5ml spoon (½ level teaspoon) salt
75g (3oz) dessicated coconut
Cold water to mix
Beaten egg or milk to glaze

**Filling**
1 × 15ml spoon (1 level tablespoon) powdered gelatine
2 eggs
250ml (½ pint) milk
2 × 15ml spoons (2 tablespoons) dark rum
1 × 15ml spoon (1 level tablespoon) cocoa
100g (4oz) castor sugar
75ml (3 fluid oz) double cream
1 × 15ml spoon (1 tablespoon) milk
Vanilla essence

---

**1.** Prepare a moderately hot oven (200 deg C, 400 deg F, Gas Mark 6).
**2.** Place flour and salt in a bowl. Add fats, cut into small pieces, and rub in with the fingertips until mixture resembles fine breadcrumbs, stir in coconut.
**3.** Add about 2 × 15ml spoons (2 tablespoons) of water and mix with a fork to form a firm dough. Turn out on to a 21.5cm (8½in) pie plate, allowing pastry to overlap rim of plate by 2·5cm (1in). Turn overlapping pastry under to give a double thickness of pastry on rim. Cut up edge with the back of a knife to form flakes and flute edge with the fingers.
**5.** Bake blind for 30 minutes. To bake blind: line pastry case with circle of greaseproof paper; fill with baking beans or rice. Place on second shelf from top of oven for 20 minutes. Remove from oven, lift out paper and beans or rice. Reduce heat to moderate (180 deg

C, 350 deg F, Gas Mark 4). Brush fluted pastry edge with beaten egg or milk.

6. Return pastry case to oven for a further 10 to 15 minutes. Leave until cold.

7. While pastry case is cooling, prepare filling. Place gelatine in a bowl. Separate eggs and add yolks to bowl; place whites in a clean greasefree bowl; place in fridge.

8. Add milk, rum and cocoa to bowl. Place bowl over a saucepan of simmering water and stir until mixture has thickened slightly and just coats the back of a spoon. Allow mixture to cool, then place in fridge until just on the point of setting.

9. Whisk egg whites until stiff, but not dry; whisk in sugar, a little at a time until all the sugar has been incorporated.

10. Place cream, milk and a few drops of vanilla essence in a bowl. Whisk until cream stands in soft peaks. Fold egg whites into chocolate mixture, cutting through mixture with a metal spoon; pour into pastry case.

11. Top with a layer of cream and swirl mixtures together with a spoon to give a marbled effect.

12. To freeze: open freeze until firm then cover with foil and store for up to 2 months. Thaw slowly in refrigerator.

## APRICOT PARFAIT PIE

### Biscuit base
200g (8oz) digestive biscuits
50g (2oz) mixed shelled nuts
2×15ml spoon (2 level tablespoons) golden syrup
50g (2oz) butter

### Filling
1 large 425g (15oz) can apricot halves
1×15ml spoon (1 level tablespoon) powdered gelatine
1 large 439g (15½oz) can rice pudding
1 packet orange Quick-Jel
Toasted flaked almonds

1. To make biscuit base: place biscuits between 2 sheets of greaseproof paper; crush finely with a rolling pin. Finely chop nuts. Measure golden syrup carefully, levelling off spoon with a knife and making sure there is none on underside of spoon.

2. Place syrup in a medium-sized saucepan with butter. Heat gently, stirring occasionally, until butter has melted. Remove pan from heat and stir in biscuit and nuts.

3. Spread biscuit mixture in base and up side of a 21·5cm (8½in) pie plate. Place in refrigerator to chill.

4. Drain syrup from can of apricots into a measuring jug and reserve 125ml (¼ pint). Place 3×15 ml spoons (3 tablespoons) of this syrup in a small basin in a pan of water over a moderate heat; stir until gelatine has dissolved. Stir in remaining measured syrup.

5. Pour contents of can of rice pudding into a basin with gelatine liquid. Pour mixture into prepared biscuit case. Place in refrigerator until set.

6. Make Quick-Jel as directed on packet.

7. Arrange apricot halves, cut sides downwards, on top of pie. Cover apricots with Quick-Jel glaze and sprinkle with a few flaked almonds.

Left: *Chocolate rum pie and apricot parfait pie*

## GOOSEBERRY CREAM DESSERT

*For 6 to 8 portions*

½kg (1lb) gooseberries
5×15ml (5 level tablespoons) granulated sugar
Custard powder
570ml (1 pint) milk
1 envelope powdered gelatine
1 142ml (5 fluid oz) carton double cream
1 hazelnut

1. Wash gooseberries and place in a medium-sized saucepan with sugar and 1×15ml spoon (1 tablespoon) water. Cook over a low heat for 15 to 20 minutes until fruit is soft. Leave to cool.

2. Make up custard as directed on packet using milk, but use 5 × 15ml spoons (5 level tablespoons) custard powder and omit sugar. Cover and leave to cool.

3. Measure 3 × 15ml spoons (3 tablespoons) water into a small basin; add gelatine and stir. Place basin in a pan of water over a moderate heat; stir until gelatine has dissolved.

4. Make a purée from fruit (press through a sieve or liquidise in an electric blender, then strain). Mix together purée, custard and gelatine.

5. Whip cream until it just holds its shape. Place 1 heaped tablespoon in a nylon piping bag fitted with a star tube; reserve in refrigerator for decoration. Stir remaining cream into fruit mixture.

6. Pour into a 1 litre (2 pint) mould or pudding basin; leave to set in refrigerator for 3 to 4 hours or overnight.

7. To unmould: Dip mould in a bowl of hand-hot water. Invert on to a serving plate; remove mould. Pipe the reserved cream in a whirl on top of the mould and decorate the cream whirl with a hazelnut.

## STRAWBERRY WHIRLS

*Makes 6*

**Biscuits**
200g (8oz) margarine
50g (2oz) castor sugar
200g (8oz) plain flour

**Filling**
200g (8oz) strawberries
200g (8oz) cream cheese
Icing sugar
Vanilla essence

1. Prepare a moderate oven (180 deg C, 350 deg F, Gas Mark 4). Grease a baking sheet. Cream margarine and sugar together until light and fluffy. Add flour and mix. Place mixture in a nylon piping bag fitted with a large star tube.

2. Pipe 12 whirls on a baking sheet, allowing room for spreading. Bake in centre of oven for 10 to 15 minutes until golden brown. Leave to cool on a baking sheet.

3. Wash strawberries, dry on kitchen paper. Reserve 6 for decoration and remove hulls from remaining strawberries; cut strawberries into quarters. Place cheese and 2 × 15ml spoons (1 rounded tablespoon) icing sugar in a bowl and beat until light and creamy; add a few drops of vanilla essence. Just before serving, fold strawberries into cheese mixture and use to sandwich biscuits together.

4. Sprinkle the top of each whirl with a little icing sugar. Use reserved strawberries to decorate the top of each whirl.

## REDCURRANT CHEESECAKE

*For 6 portions*

200g (8oz) digestive biscuits
2×15ml spoons (2 level tablespoons) golden syrup
100g (4oz) butter
1 medium-sized lemon
200g (8oz) cream cheese
50g (2oz) castor sugar
1×2·5ml spoon (½ teaspoon) vanilla essence
¼kg (8oz) redcurrants
3×15ml spoons (3 level tablespoons) granulated sugar
1×10ml spoon (1 rounded teaspoon) cornflour

1. Lightly grease a 20·5cm (8in) loose based cake tin with melted fat or oil. Place biscuits between 2 sheets of greaseproof paper; crush finely with a rolling pin.

2. Measure the golden syrup carefully, levelling off spoon with a knife, and making sure there is none on the underside of spoon. Place in a medium-sized saucepan with butter. Heat gently, stirring occasionally until butter has melted; remove pan from heat and stir in biscuits. Press mixture on base and about 4cm (1½in) up side of tin.

3. Scrub lemon; grate rind and squeeze juice. Place cream cheese, castor sugar and vanilla essence in a bowl; beat until smooth. Add lemon rind and juice; pour into biscuit base and leave to set in refrigerator for 3 to 4 hours or overnight.

4. Reserve 6 small sprigs of redcurrants for decoration. Remove stalks from remainder, wash well and place in a medium-sized saucepan with granulated sugar and 4×15ml spoons (4 tablespoons) water. Bring to boil and simmer gently for 5 to 10 minutes until fruit is soft; cool. Strain fruit; reserve juice.

5. Place cornflour in a saucepan, blend with a little water, add juice and bring to boil, stirring. Arrange fruit over top of cheesecake, brush with thickened juice to glaze.

6. Remove cheesecake from tin by placing on top of a 450g (1lb) can and gently pulling down tin from cheesecake. Ease cheesecake off base with a palette knife and place on a serving plate. Decorate with reserved fruit.

## RED FRUIT KISSEL
*For 3 to 4 portions*

---

450g (½lb) mixed red fruits
raspberries, blackcurrants,
redcurrants, etc.)
2×15ml spoons (2 level
tablespoons) cornflour
½×2·5ml spoon (¼ level teaspoon)
ground cinnamon
4×15ml (2 rounded tablespoons)
granulated sugar
1 medium-sized orange
Castor sugar
1 small carton single cream

---

1. Wash fruit; remove any leaves, stalks and hulls. Place cornflour, cinnamon and sugar in a saucepan. Blend in 125ml (¼ pint) water.
2. Using a sharp knife or vegetable peeler, peel thin strips of orange peel for decoration.
3. Squeeze juice from orange and add to pan with fruit. Bring to boil, stirring gently, and simmer for 1 minute, or until fruit is soft, but not broken. Leave to cool.
4. Divide the kissel between 3 or 4 glasses, sprinkle each with a little castor sugar to prevent a skin forming; chill. To serve, top each kissel with a little cream. Place an orange peel strip on each glass and serve any remaining cream separately.

*Right, clockwise from top: Gooseberry cream dessert, red fruit kissel, redcurrant cheesecake, loganberry pancakes, strawberry whirls, gooseberry water ice, raspberry flan*

---

## SUMMER RASPBERRY FLAN
*For 6 portions*

---

**Pastry**
100g (4oz) plain flour
1×15ml (1 level tablespoon)
castor sugar
½×2·5ml spoon (¼ level teaspoon)
salt
25g (1oz) margarine
25g (1oz) lard
1 egg yolk

**Filling**
1 egg
50g (2oz) castor sugar
25g (1oz) plain flour
250ml (½ pint) milk
1×2·5ml spoon (½ teaspoon)
vanilla essence
25g (1oz) butter

**Topping**
1 egg white
50g (2oz) castor sugar
100g (4oz) raspberries
4×15ml spoon (4 level
tablespoons) raspberry jam

---

1. Prepare a moderate oven (180 deg C, 350 deg F, Gas Mark 4). Place a 20·5cm (8in) fluted flan ring on a baking sheet.
2. Sift flour, castor sugar and salt in a bowl; add fats, cut into small pieces and rub in with fingertips until the mixture resembles fine breadcrumbs. Add egg yolk and 2 to 3 × 5ml spoons (2 to 3 teaspoons) of water to form a firm dough.
3. Turn out on to a floured board and knead lightly. Roll out to a circle 4cm (1½in) larger all round than the flan ring. Support pastry over rolling pin and lift on to flan ring. Press pastry into flutes with the finger. Roll off surplus pastry with rolling pin across top of flan ring. Press pastry into flutes again; prick base of flan with a fork.
4. Place a circle of greaseproof paper in flan and fill with baking beans. Bake in centre of oven for 15 minutes; remove paper and beans and cook for 5 minutes. Leave to cool; remove flan ring.
5. To make filling: place egg and sugar in a bowl and whisk until thick. Add flour and 15ml (1 table-spoon) of the measured milk; whisk well.
6. Boil remaining milk; whisk into egg mixture. Return to saucepan; bring to boil whisking continuously. Cook 2 minutes; beat in vanilla essence and butter then pour into flan case.
7. Prepare a moderate oven (190 deg C, 375 deg F, Gas Mark 5). Place egg white in a clean, grease-free bowl and whisk until stiff but not dry. Whisk in half the sugar, then fold in the remainder, cutting through the mixture with a metal spoon until all the sugar has been incorporated.
8. Place meringue in a nylon piping bag fitted with a medium-sized plain tube. Pipe meringue around edge of flan and bake in centre of oven for 5 to 10 minutes until golden brown.
9. Arrange fruit in centre of flan. Place jam with 2 × 15ml spoons (2 tablespoons) water in a small saucepan over a low heat and warm until the jam has melted. Sieve warmed jam into a basin and pour over raspberries to glaze.

---

## GOOSEBERRY WATER ICE
*For 4 portions*

---

200g (½lb) gooseberries
50g (2oz) granulated sugar
Green food colouring, optional

---

1. Turn refrigerator to coldest setting. Wash fruit and remove any stalks or leaves. Place in a medium-sized saucepan with sugar and 125ml (¼ pint) water.
2. Bring to boil, cover and simmer for 15 to 20 minutes until fruit is soft. Leave to cool. Make a purée (press through a sieve, or liquidise in an electric blender), then strain. Add a few drops of colouring, if desired.
3. Pour purée into a small plastic or metal dish (or empty ice tray, if sections can be removed). Freeze for 2½ to 3 hours until firm. Turn refrigerator back to normal setting. Serve with sugar biscuits.

## LOGANBERRY PANCAKES

100g (4oz) plain flour
a pinch of salt
1 egg
250ml ($\frac{1}{2}$ pint) milk
Oil or white fat for frying

### Topping

$\frac{1}{4}$kg (8oz) loganberries
4×15ml spoon (4 level
    tablespoons) castor sugar
Flaked almonds
1×142ml (5 fluid oz) carton
    double cream
1×10ml spoon (2 teaspoons)
    icing sugar
1×5ml spoon (1 teaspoon)
    ground ginger

1. Place flour and salt in a mixing bowl. Make a well in centre of flour and add egg. Stir in half the milk gradually, mix well and beat until smooth. Add remaining milk then pour into a jug.

2. Heat a little oil or fat in a medium-sized frying pan. Pour off any excess fat into a small bowl, leaving pan lightly greased. Stir batter and pour sufficient into pan, swirling quickly to coat surface thinly. Cook until underside is golden.

3. Hold pan over a sheet of greaseproof paper and slip pancake to side of pan opposite handle. Toss or flip over with a palette knife.

4. Cook pancake over a moderate heat until second side is brown. Invert pancake on to a sheet of greaseproof paper. Keep in a warm oven. Use remaining batter to make more pancakes.

5. Wash loganberries if necessary; dry on kitchen paper. Place in a bowl with sugar, and turn to coat. Remove rack from grill, place almonds in pan and lightly toast nuts. Place cream, icing sugar and ginger in a bowl and whip until cream just holds its shape.

6. Just before serving, fold pancakes into quarters and arrange on a warmed serving plate. Place loganberries in folds of each pancake and top with ginger cream. Sprinkle cream with almonds and serve immediately.

# Buying and storing food

By buying sensibly and by making the most of your oven whenever you use it, you can save both time and money. But for this to be successful, you must also know how to store food properly, whether it's fresh, frozen, canned or dried.

## Shopping and Food Hints

1. Buy foods when in season.
2. Shop around for the best prices and buy in bulk or in large sizes wherever possible.
3. Make a shopping list and keep to it.
4. Try to plan two or three days' menus in advance, bearing in mind the possible use of leftovers.
5. Foods sold loose are cheaper than packaged foods.
6. Cheaper cuts of meat are just as tasty and nutritious as the more expensive cuts. They are not so tender, but this can be overcome by long, slow cooking.
7. Cheese, weight for weight, is more nutritious than meat. It is quicker to prepare, and is just as versatile. Serve cheese for at least one main meal and one supper dish each week, to add variety to your menus.
8. Eggs are reasonable most of the year and may also be included in the weekly diet, as well as being served for breakfast and high teas.
9. Soups made at home are good fillers, besides being cheap. Use root vegetables and rice, spaghetti, pearl barley or lentils. Bones can be used from the joint or bought cheaply. The flavour can be enhanced by the addition of a little meat or meat extract. For a more substantial meal, serve with small dumplings.
10. The less expensive varieties of margarine and lard are just as good as the more expensive ones for most cooking purposes.
11. Cakes should be made at home. For a change, use dripping in place of margarine for a rich fruit cake; this gives an excellent flavour. Make a large batch of cake mixture and divide to make a large cake, buns and fruit pudding, varying the flavourings.
12. Make a large quantity of pastry at a time; store rubbed-in pastry in a covered jar for two to three weeks in the refrigerator. Moisten with water and roll out as required. For a richer dough, mix with an egg. Alternatively, just stir in sugar and use for a crumble topping.
13. When using the oven for a casserole or joint, be sure to bake a cake or pudding at the same time, or cook vegetables in the oven to serve with the meat.

## Everyday Menu Planning

To be able to budget wisely, it is necessary to plan menus ahead, and it's helpful to plan a week at a time. It is then possible to offset the cost of an expensive meal with a cheaper one, and to make use of left-overs. Nutritionally, too, it is important, as over a week it's possible to include all the essential foods. Each day's meals must have a well-balanced proportion of each food type. Serve meat, eggs, fish or cheese once a day and make sure that all the family drink some milk (especially younger children). These are the protein foods that are essential for growth and repair. Pulses, such as lentils and split peas, are rich in protein and economical. Each day, serve a green vegetable or salad and fresh fruit, including some citrus fruit. Serve bread, cakes and breakfast cereals as appetite satisfiers—they contain some essential vitamins and mineral elements. Sugar and sweet foods are essential for giving energy. However, if more sugar is eaten than can be used, the excess is stored as fat. Limit the amount of sweet foods in a menu, and avoid between-meal sweets. Give children apples and carrots instead: they're much better for their teeth, too.

When planning your menus, bear in mind the following points:

1. **Avoid monotony:** Don't serve up the same food too often. Meals quickly become dull, if the same flavour keeps appearing. This, of course, excludes staple foods, like bread or potatoes.

2. **Planning each meal:** Decide first upon the protein content—whether to serve meat, fish, eggs or cheese, then choose the dairy foods, fruit and vegetables and, finally, the carbohydrate foods, such as potatoes, bread, cakes and sugar.

3. **Variety:** When planning meals, take into account the colour, flavour and texture of the foods to be served, so that they complement each other: make sure that dishes look attractive, serve a soft food with a crunchy one, a bland dish with one that is highly seasoned.

4. **Accompaniments:** Serve pickles, chutneys and ketchup to pep up bland foods, and make use of inexpensive garnishes.

## Using Your Refrigerator

The correct temperature for the main part of the refrigerator is 4 to 7 deg C (40 to 47 deg F). As the atmosphere in a refrigerator is dry, and moisture is evaporated from any exposed surface, food must be wrapped in polythene bags or foil, or put in covered containers. Jugs of liquid, especially milk, must be covered with a 'cap' of foil. Meat should be loosely wrapped or stored in containers without a tight seal, to allow some air to circulate. Wrapping prevents flavours from one food passing to another. Dairy foods are particularly prone to absorption of stronger flavours. See the chart for details.

The coldest part of a refrigerator is at the top, immediately below the ice-making compartment. Highly perishable foods, such as prepared meats, poultry and fish must be placed at the top, and salad vegetables at the bottom (see chart). All food must be cold before it is put in the refrigerator. Do not overload the shelves, for effective refrigeration depends upon the proper circulation of air inside the cabinet.

The length of storage time varies with the type of food, and also depends on how fresh it is when put into the refrigerator: check storage times with the chart.

Fresh fruit need not be refrigerated unless the ripening process is to be retarded. Melons and pineapples should not be put in the refrigerator unless carefully covered, or their strong smell will contaminate other foods, and they should be left only for a very short time. Bananas will blacken if refrigerated. Eggs should be stored, pointed end downwards, well away from the freezing compartment. If they are needed for boiling, mayonnaise, or cake making, they must be left out to come to room temperature before use—or keep some in the kitchen cupboard.

Wilting lettuce can be revived in the refrigerator. Prepare, wash and shake off surplus water, and place loosely in a tightly covered container. Leave for several hours. Keep mayonnaise in a tightly covered container for up to three weeks. Chill cream before whipping to get a better volume.

## Buying and Storing Frozen Food

Frozen foods, once thawed, begin to lose flavour and texture in the same way as other fresh foods. Storage time varies with the degree of cold in your storage compartment, for although all compartments freeze water quite successfully, the actual temperature in different models varies from −18 deg C (0 deg F) to about −6 deg C (21 deg F). The colder the temperature, the longer foods keep.

To be sure that frozen food is in good condition, check that foods are stacked below the load line before purchasing. Refuse any packet that feels soft or wet. Frozen food is unlikely to thaw out for an hour or so while you bring it home. Even if the packet has softened a little on the outside, it can still be put into the storage compartment. Only when the packet is completely thawed is there likely to be any deterioration in quality if it is re-frozen.

## Storing Canned and Dried Foods

Canned foods should be stored in a cool, dry place; damp storage will cause rusting which may lead to perforation and spoilage of the contents. The date of purchase should be marked on the cans and they should be used in rotation. Canned meat and fish in oil will keep for up to five years, vegetables for two years, fruit and milk for one year. If a can is opened and the contents are not completely used, the remainder will keep as long as

## Maximum Storage Time for Foods in Refrigerator

| Food | Preparation | Position in Cabinet | Time in Days |
|------|-------------|---------------------|--------------|
| Butter, margarine and cooking fats | Keep wrapped in packets; cover if on dish | Door or near bottom | 3 to 7 |
| Milk, cream, yoghourt and cottage cheese | Keep covered | Door or near bottom | 3 to 7 |
| Hard cheese | Keep loosely wrapped | Bottom | 21 |
| Eggs | On racks provided; remove two hours before using for boiling or cakes | Door or at bottom | 7 to 10 |
| Fish | Wipe with kitchen paper; cover loosely | Top or in chill tray | 1 to 2 |
| Meat, poultry and bacon joints | Wipe with kitchen paper; cover with foil or polythene | Top | Meat: 4 to 5 Bacon: 10 to 12 Poultry: 2 to 3 |
| Minced raw meat | Place in non-airtight container | Top | 1 to 3 |
| Offal | Place in non-airtight container | Top | 1 |
| Sliced bacon | Place in non-airtight container or wrap loosely | Top | 7 to 10 |
| Sausages | Keep in original wrappings or place in polythene bag | Top | From butcher: 3 Branded packs: 7 |
| Cooked sliced meats | Wrap or place in covered container | Centre | 2 to 6 according to type |
| Salads and green vegetables | Prepare ready for use. Wash, drain and wrap loosely in polythene bags or foil, or place in container provided | Bottom | 3 to 7 |
| Soft fruit | Remove any bad fruit, sprinkle with sugar and place in covered container | Centre | 1 to 3 |

cooked food in the refrigerator. Unused canned fruit or fruit juices left in the tin once opened alter slightly in flavour, so empty any left-overs into a dish.

Dehydrated foods should be stored in a well-ventilated, cool, dry and dark place, as air, heat and moisture can cause deterioration. They can be stored for twelve months. Once a packet is opened, however, it must be used within a week. Dry foods such as flour, rice and pulses, should not be put away in paper bags or opened cartons. Glass jars are ideal as the contents can be easily checked. Plastic tops are preferable to metal screw tops if there is any possibility of the store becoming damp from steam in the kitchen. Never put new supplies on top of older ones.

Keep new packets unopened in a cool, dry cupboard until required. When storage jar is empty, wash well and dry thoroughly.

## Storing Jams, Jellies, Pickles and Chutneys

Choose a cool, dark cupboard and check jars regularly. If opened jars of jam and jelly start to foment, store them in the refrigerator.

# Using a freezer

Freezer owners—like squirrels—can have a hoard of food always at the ready. If you have to go out and leave a meal for the family, run out of bread or milk, or have a surplus of fresh or cooked food, the freezer really comes into its own.

Freezing is the simplest, most natural method of preserving as the food is not altered in any way. It is a perfectly safe method, too, as organisms that otherwise destroy food stay dormant at very low temperatures. Food will not pick up any food-poisoning bacteria in a freezer, although it will deteriorate in flavour and texture if the temperature is allowed to rise in the freezer, or if its packaging is not moisture-proof.

Food will not keep for ever, of course. Most food has a storage life; uncooked food generally keeps longer than made-up dishes. Most foods will freeze successfully, the exceptions being the very juicy foods like cucumber and tomatoes. The white of hard-boiled egg toughens, and should not be used in sandwiches which are to be frozen. Bananas blacken if frozen.

## Uses of a Home Freezer

### Storage of commercial quick-frozen food: Many savings can be made by buying in bulk at low prices. When receiving a delivery of frozen foods, quickly stack the cartons in the freezer, and use older packs first. If buying food from a shop, it's useful to have an insulated bag with a frozen sachet, to keep the frozen packs cold while you are transporting them. The conservator type of cabinet—designed to stay at −18 deg C (0 deg F)—is suitable for storing all commercially frozen foods.

### Freezing of garden produce, surplus food or home-cooked food: A freezer that will maintain a temperature of −21 deg C (−5 deg F) or below is essential for freezing food at home. Check the manufacturer's instruction booklet to find out how much food can be frozen at one time; it is usually one-tenth of the capacity of the freezer in every twenty-four hours. Freeze food as soon as it's available and as quickly as possible, to retain its quality. Each package being frozen must be in contact with the freezer shelf or the coldest part of the freezer. Stack packages singly until they are frozen, when they may be placed on top of one another in a different part of the freezer. Food for freezing must be fresh and in perfect condition; it will deteriorate in flavour and texture if the temperature is too high during storage.

## Freezer Packaging

The atmosphere in a freezer is very drying, and food must be covered completely in moisture-proof, vapour-proof materials to avoid 'freezer burn', which causes discoloration and dried-out patches. Thick polythene, thick (heavy duty) foil and waxed or plastic cartons must be used. Bags and wrapping papers are available from specialist suppliers or stationers. Shallow containers are preferable to deep ones, as the food freezes and subsequently thaws more quickly. Air must be removed from the container—whatever the type—to prevent deterioration of the food.

### Polythene bags: Thick gusseted bags are best. Use for bulky items such as bread and joints of meat. Carefully press out all air before sealing with a plastic-coated metal tag or pipe cleaner, or by knotting the bag. Overwrap awkwardly shaped packages with brown paper or mutton cloth to avoid the polythene being pierced when the food is moved around in the freezer. Use polythene bags to line cardboard cartons when freezing liquids.

### Plastic boxes: Although quite expensive to buy, these last for years and are very easy to use, especially those with special air-tight lid seals. Use special freezer tape for sealing the lids on the rigid boxes. Ordinary clear adhesive will not withstand the low temperature. Use plastic boxes for liquids, stews, fruit, vegetables and sauces. Allow a small space at

the top when filling, for the food to expand when frozen. Utilise well-washed cartons that food has been bought in.

**Labelling:** It is most important to label everything clearly, stating the nature of the food, the number of portions, the date, and any information needed when the food comes to be used. Write with a waxed crayon or felt-tipped pen and use special freezer labels or labels covered with transparent freezer tape. One type of freezer tape is opaque and can be written on. Luggage labels are useful for tying to polythene bags: different coloured ones can be used to denote meat, fish, or vegetables. Keep a list of the food in the freezer.

## General Rules for Freezing

Use only good-quality food in peak condition and handle it as little as possible. Keep everything very clean, to avoid introducing harmful bacteria into the food. Freeze cooked food as soon as possible after preparation, first cooling it in ice-cold water, then in the refrigerator. Protect food well during storage. Seasoning and flavourings used develop during storage, so use these in moderation.

## Making the Most of your Freezer

Make pastry, roll it out to the shape of your pie dish and place it between layers of foil; overwrap with foil and freeze for the time when you want to make a pie. Prepare individual dishes for any member of the family on a diet or for separate meals when you are going to be away. Baby foods can be prepared and frozen in small containers.

Store any left-overs for future use. Keep a loaf of bread and a carton of homogenised milk in the freezer for use in emergencies. Sliced bread can be toasted while still frozen.

Prepare food in advance for parties, picnics and special occasions. Batch baking will always save time.

# Index